TIME TO STARE

What is this life if, full of care,
We have no time to stand and stare.

No time to stand beneath the boughs
And stare as long as sheep or cows.

No time to see, when woods we pass,
Where squirrels hide their nuts in grass.

No time to see, in broad daylight,
Streams full of stars like stars at night.

No time to turn at Beauty's glance
And watch her feet, how they can dance.

No time to wait till her mouth can
Enrich that smile her eyes began.

A poor life this if, full of care,
We have no time to stand and stare.

Poem *Leisure* by W.H. DAVIES

Ray Armstrong

ACKNOWLEDGEMENT

First I must thank my wife and son who have encouraged and supported me throughout the book's long gestation and difficult birth.

I am also very grateful to Julian Branscombe of the Gwent Wildlife Trust for his support and for the representatives of the late W.H. Davies for allowing me to publish some of his poems, one of which *Leisure*, inspired me to the title *Time to Stare*.

Published by

Grice Chapman Publishing

The Shire House, Burgh next Aylsham
Norwich, NR11 6TP

www.gricechapman.com

Grice Chapman is a division of Evergreen Media

ISBN 0-9545726-6-1

Designed and printed in England by
Barnwell's Print Ltd, Printing Works
2-6 Penfold Street, Aylsham, Norfolk, NR11 6ET
Telephone: +44 (0)1263 732767

Right: Woodland birds (great spotted woodpecker, nuthatch and treecreeper)

Preface

I am really pleased to be able to offer a preface for 'Time to Stare'. Ray Armstrong's dazzlingly-illustrated account of 25 years of wildlife observations in a small tract of eastern Monmouthshire really brings this part of Wales to life – and this relatively-little known area is full of treasures.

This area, which includes the Trellech Plateau and the neighbouring Wye Valley, has been one of the richest surprises for me in my travels around the country. I was lucky enough to be taken to the Gwent Wildlife Trust reserve of New Grove Meadows, just north of Trellech – and beautifully featured in Ray's book – a couple of years ago to film for my 'Special Reserves' programme. The sight of tens of thousands of orchids framing a stunning vista across South Wales made such an impression on me.

It is wonderful to read of someone who knows their local patch so well. I can really relate to the enjoyment of going out again and again, through all seasons and all weathers and from year to year, to enjoy favourite sites and find new ones.

I am deeply jealous of many of the species and habitats that Ray has on his patch. I have yet to see an amazing beetle called the bee chafer *Trichius hispidus*. Very few naturalists have seen this distinctive beetle, although the notebooks of the Alfred Russell Wallace, and colleague of Charles Darwin in the discovery of evolution, show that a Monmouthshire naturalist of an earlier era was also lucky enough to get to know this special creature. Ray has not only seen the insect, but has captured it on film so well that my desire to chase this beast down is only heightened.

As a winner in the recent Wildlife Trust's Natural World Wales wildlife photography competition, Ray's pictures are getting known by many. To see so many gorgeous shots in one beautifully produced book is a real treat.

Ray's work is full of poignant reminders of the changes that our countryside has faced. Some of these – such as the return of the polecat to Monmouthshire – are to be welcomed, but all too many are a concern. A pub on the Trellech ridge was called The Gocket – a local name for the black grouse. The closure of this local pub echoes the loss of these fine birds from this area. Thankfully I can still find these totemic birds in the hills around my mid-Wales home.

The decision of Ray and the publishers to support the work of the Welsh Wildlife Trusts through publication of this book is to be applauded. It is through the work of naturalists such as Ray combined with effective conservation organisations such as the Wildlife Trusts and wildlife-loving farmers that we can secure the deserved future for our magnificent wildlife and countryside.

Iolo Williams
Broadcaster & Naturalist
Powys, 12 May 2005

Above: New Grove Meadows - a breathtaking wildflower and scenic treasure
Right: Bargain Wood - 'Mother Nature' in all her glory

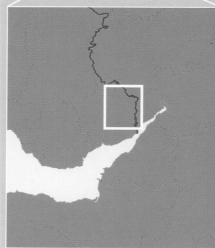

N

The broken line
encompasses the area
of interest.

OS Map scale: 1:25 000

Contents

Introduction

Throughout history, wildlife in Britain has been dependent on the farmland and forest environment. As the countryside experiences evolutionary changes, either fashioned by the hand of man or naturally as the result of climatic change, so does the resident wildlife. Some species will move away, whilst others will move in, as different habitats are generated.

Birds are particularly vulnerable to changes in the environment, especially as a result of farming methods that jeopardise their nesting sites. In coniferous woodlands, cyclical felling and tree replanting programmes generate a myriad of changing habitats that affect both the type of species present and their numbers. Although harvesting of a forest crop dramatically alters the habitat, it need not destroy it, particularly when it is carried out with sensitivity to ensure there are always trees at different stages of development.

For 25 years I have taken a keen interest in the wildlife in a small Area of Outstanding Natural Beauty in East Monmouthshire, one of Britain's most picturesque counties. This book presents a complete review of all the birds and animals that can be seen in the area together with an overview of the most interesting and photogenic insects.

My own affinity with the countryside and its wildlife stems from my upbringing on a farm in an era when the pace of life was more leisurely and people were more aware of the natural world around them.

The village primary school I attended played a huge part in encouraging my interest in wildlife. Nature study walks were some of the highlights of the spring and summer terms. There were always glass tanks in the classroom containing some form of wildlife, ranging from tadpoles and newts to various species of munching

A view across the heather covered Cleddon Bog

caterpillars. All the children used to take turns in feeding the residents, changing the water, and cleaning the tanks.

Most of the pupil's parents were associated with the land in some way, and so our out-of-school interests were usually nature orientated. Like other children, I used to walk to and from school across fields and along tree and hedge-lined country lanes alive with wildlife. On the farm I recall watching boxing hares, which were common then. I saw and heard birds like the corncrake and corn bunting.

How things have changed! The latest census suggests the British hare population has fallen by more than 75 per cent in the last 60 years. The migrant corncrake disappeared from mainland Britain as a breeding species in the latter half of the 20th century. It now breeds only in the Western Isles, but the Royal Society for the Protection of Birds is involved in conservation work aimed at its re-introduction into certain parts of the country. The resident cirl bunting has also suffered a marked decline, and now only breeds in South Devon.

I remember being shown wonderfully camouflaged

nidifugous lapwing chicks squatting motionless in the grass while the parent birds wheeled overhead, calling and trying to lure us away. I recall once finding the nest of a red-backed shrike, a bird which no longer breeds in Britain. The last confirmed breeding was in Scotland in 1999.

Dormice are now rare, but were commonplace in the hedgerows. Their nests were often found by farm workers when they were hedge-laying and ditching; they would then show them to their children. For any young child to see and possibly hold a dormouse, one of our most endearing indigenous animals, is an unforgettable experience.

For me all these experiences and discoveries were magical and are indelibly printed in my psyche. Yet we now live in an age of extinction. The Red List of Threatened Species compiled by the World Conservation Union - a body that brings together governments, environmental activists, scientists and business - lists nearly 16,000 species as being under threat. More than 200 of them are already described as 'possibly extinct', and almost 3,000 as 'critically endangered'. The earth is currently losing species at a rate comparable to the mass extinction of the dinosaur. I think it is incumbent on the public to pressurise governments to do all that is possible to safeguard our wildlife which gives us so much pleasure.

As a teenager, I used to help on the farm, and one of my favourite jobs in the spring was to harrow and roll the grass fields and winter-sown cereals, often the site of nesting lapwings. I always kept a sharp look out for the nests and on finding one I would jump off the tractor, move the eggs to one side, drive over the nest and then replace the eggs. Watching the parent bird return to the nest, as if nothing had happened, was a source of great satisfaction. When I look back, I realise that this early encouragement to use my eyes not only highlighted the wonders of nature but also probably subconsciously taught me the merits of awareness and attention to detail, which are very important in our everyday lives.

All these memories and interests were reawakened in 1975 when we moved to live in the scenic Monmouthshire countryside. This book brings together my observations over the subsequent years together with a selection of the photographs I have taken along the way. It seemed to me words were not capable of fully describing the natural beauty of our native wildlife, and, as they say, 'a picture paints a thousand words'. I must also add that this book would not have been possible without the friendly co-operation of all the local farmers who allowed me to wander at will across their land.

Over the past quarter century I have witnessed a marked reduction in the population of certain resident species of birds, namely bullfinch, Eurasian curlew, goldcrest, house sparrow, kestrel, lesser spotted woodpecker, linnet, little owl, marsh tit, mistle thrush, northern lapwing, yellowhammer, song thrush, starling, skylark, tree sparrow and willow tit.

On the positive side I should add that the song thrush numbers have increased over the last couple of years. The reasons for these reductions are numerous, complex and, in the case of some species, interrelated. They include climate changes, overuse of pesticides, and habitat loss like the removal of hedges, the draining of wet areas, barn conversions, cleaner farmyards and changes in farming practices. The move from hay to silage over recent years - and the associated multiple grass cuttings over the spring and early summer months - has resulted in nest losses and the inevitable reduction in numbers of the ground-nesting skylark and Eurasian curlew.

But a significant factor in the small bird losses is, in my opinion, the large increase in a number of predatory species in the area such as carrion crows, magpies and Eurasian jays. All these corvids are renowned nest robbers. Carrion crow numbers in particular have increased dramatically. If, in the past, you saw a flock of large black birds in a field you immediately knew they were rooks, as carrion crows were only seen in pairs or in small family groups. This is no longer the case. Flocks of 30-50 carrion crows are now commonplace.

My observations have shown that nest robbing and the predation of young fledglings by corvids occurs regularly along the woodland edges, as well as in old hedges with integrated mature trees. A further threat to nesting birds in these same places comes from the ubiquitous grey squirrel, a known predator of birds eggs and nestlings, whose numbers have also increased markedly in the past 10 years. Their presence is

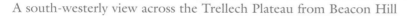

A south-westerly view across the Trellech Plateau from Beacon Hill

emphasised by the number that fall victim to traffic on the minor roads nearby, particularly those that run along the woodland edge.

I think there is now a strong case for a national programme of selective culling of both the carrion crow and the grey squirrel, an animal that also does considerable damage to trees of all ages.

Similarly, over this period of time the numbers of certain summer visitors have also declined - namely the barn swallow, common redstart, cuckoo, pied flycatcher, spotted flycatcher, tree pipit, turtle dove, willow warbler and wood warbler. The common redstart, pied flycatcher, wood warbler, spotted flycatcher and turtle dove must now be considered scarce locally. The reason for their decline is in general the same as stated earlier, but in the case of certain species there is the added loss due to shooting and netting whilst on migration. Despite attempts to stop these traditional pursuits, they still continue in a number of Mediterranean countries.

Yet, despite these pressures, only one species has been totally lost to the district and that is the grasshopper warbler, never common, it disappeared in the early 1980s. About the same time we lost the reed bunting as a breeding species, it now only appears very occasionally in early spring and then moves on. But there are real fears for the survival in the area of the resident little owl and lesser spotted woodpecker as well as the summer-visiting pied flycatcher, common redstart, wood warbler, turtle dove and spotted flycatcher. To counteract this I am happy to state that we have gained the elegant yellow wagtail, a trans-Saharan migrant. To my knowledge, it first nested here in 1997 and one or two pairs have since returned every year. However, I think its long-term survival locally is tenuous, as its numbers are declining nationally. On the furry front, the polecat has recently returned after a long period of absence.

The area covers approximately 20 square km of farmland and Forestry Commission woodland that hide a variety of habitats. The farms are mainly livestock based, but, over the last decade, there has been a shift towards arable agriculture. The largest tracts of farmland are in the western sector centred on the village of Trellech in an area called the Trellech Plateau, which is at an altitude of 215 metres falling away to 170 metres at Hygga and Hygga Dingle in the south. In the south-east the land falls away to 105 metres at Botany Bay where the narrow, babbling Cat Brook, whose source is near Catbrook village, runs under the road in two places before continuing its journey downhill to join the River Wye at Tintern.

The woodland that covers roughly a quarter of the district dominates the rising ground to the north and east of Trellech, and forms part of the Tintern Forest, rising to 307 metres on Beacon Hill on the rim of the Wye Valley. Here tree felling over the last 10 years has opened up spectacular panoramic views, the panorama running from the distant Black Mountains, highlighted by the graphically named Sugar Loaf and Brecon Beacons in the west, round to the South Cotswold Hills in Gloucestershire in the east. The woods are mainly coniferous, but there are some areas of deciduous trees, together with a few pockets of mixed woodland. The most expansive deciduous woods are Manor Wood in the north-east where **wild daffodils** *(Narcissus pseudonarcissus)* can be seen on the woodland floor in spring, and Bargain Wood and Creigiau Wood, which extend from the village of Cleddon to Botany Bay in the south-east corner of the area. Many of the woods support beautiful displays of **bluebells** *(Hyacinthoides non-scripta)* in the spring. There is also a fine display to be seen in open countryside below the Roman settlement site near Hygga. This flower, of which Britain has half the global population, was recently crowned the wildflower emblem of the United Kingdom.

Outstanding sylvan and river views can be seen from a number of viewing points in Bargain Wood. The most northerly provides a seat under the trees and a bird's-eye view of the River Wye as it flows down from Bigsweir Bridge past the village of Llandogo in the valley below.

A wonderful open display of bluebells near Hygga

When I sit under a green tree
Silent, and breathing all the while
As easy as a sleeping child
And smiling with as soft a smile.
Then, as my brains begin to work,
This is the thought that comes to me:
Were such a peace more often mine,
I'd live as long as this green tree.

From *The Tree* by the Monmouthshire poet
W.H. DAVIES

Another place which presents superb views of the steep and wooded slopes running down into the Wye Valley below is the edge of Cuckoo Wood, just south of the village of Pen-y-fan in the north-east corner. In autumn all these viewing points present wonderful views of the wooded slopes resplendently dressed in their seasonal colours; this display of autumn colours is one of the great natural splendours for which the Wye Valley is renowned.

Natural springs on the Trellech Plateau provide the source for numerous small streams that drain water from the plateau and the surrounding high ground, finding their way into the River Usk in the west, the River Trothy in the north and the River Wye in the south and east.

There are a few small permanent and seasonal ponds dotted around.

To the east is Cleddon Bog, which is the best example of a lowland bog habitat in Monmouthshire, and a rare feature in the whole of south-west Britain. The Bog, an area of eight hectares, is contained within a Site of Special Scientific Interest, which covers an area of 15 hectares. Together with the adjacent woodland it is one of the most important lepidoptrea sites in Monmouthshire. The run out from Cleddon Bog sources the waterfall at Cleddon, which can be quite spectacular following a spell of wet weather. It was near here under the sycamore trees that William Wordsworth commenced the writing of his poem *Lines*.

Five years have past; five summers, with the length
Of five long winters! And again I hear
These waters, rolling from their mountain springs
With a soft inland murmer. Once again
Do I behold these steep and lofty cliffs,
That on a wild secluded scene impress
Thoughts of more deep seclusion; and connect
The landscape with the quiet of the sky.
The day is come when I again repose
Here under this dark sycamore, and view
These plots of cottage-ground, these orchard-tufts.

WILLIAM WORDSWORTH

Autumn colour and a bird's eye view of the winding River Wye from Bargain Wood

Part One *Birds*

Birds, whether resident or summer/winter visitors, will tend to be found in their most favoured habitats. Many species will feed in one habitat and breed in a different, adjacent place, especially in newly planted areas and along the woodland edge. The smaller birds will generally feed and nest in the same habitat. However it should be noted that these favoured areas are not the only places where the birds will be found. Many birds of the woodland, woodland-edge and farmland regularly visit private gardens, particularly during the autumn and winter months, to take advantage of the food people put out for them. In certain instances, they may even nest there too.

To make identification easier, I have grouped the birds by their typical habitats and provided a cameo description of each species. The woodlands support the greatest variety of birds, and these can be separated into five types.

- Clear fell and newly planted areas, with trees up to 6 metres high

- Pole-stage plantation

- Mature coniferous forest

- Mature mixed and broad-leaved woodland

- Woodland edge.

It should be remembered that clear fell and newly planted coniferous areas do change quite rapidly and in ten years may well be unrecognisable. The rest of the birds are to be found on the mixed farmland.

Chapter 1
Clear fell and newly planted areas

When any area is clear felled and replanted, the bare earth is rapidly colonised by indigenous plants, shrubs and trees such as climbing corydalis, foxglove, bilberry, bracken, a variety of grasses, heather, gorse and silver birch, all of which will compete with the newly planted trees for sunlight, nutrients and moisture.

The seeds of **foxgloves** *(Digitalis purpurea)* have often laid dormant for years, but soil disturbance and the sudden ingress of light and warmth will trigger germination - and provide a rewarding blaze of colour and some compensation for the temporary loss of the trees. The foxglove was nominated by the public as the floral emblem for Monmouthshire in a recent survey conducted by the nature charity Plantlife.

As the plantation increases in height, suppressing the smaller plants and reducing the birds' direct access to the ground, some ground-nesting birds, like the nightjar and tree pipit will move on. This species movement whether driven by feeding or nesting requirements is an ongoing process and will continue over the life of the plantation.

It is possible to see the following birds during this particular growth phase of the plantation:

The **turtle dove** *(Streptopelia turtur)*, a summer visitor, is smaller and slimmer than a wood pigeon, with a mainly black tail, conspicuously white edged, which is markedly evident in flight. The upper-parts are chestnut with a conspicuous patch of black and white stripes on both sides of its neck. This patch is absent on young birds. The under-parts are vinous purple, passing to white. The call is a musical purring and is aptly described by the bird's Latin name *turtur* thus 'woo-tur-r-r-tur-r-r'. Repeated with minor variations, this purring song seems to add the

final soporific touch to a languid summer's day. The turtle dove is a species that is in serious decline and the Trellech/Wye Valley locality is now the only area in Wales where they breed. It is a seed eater and is particularly partial to climbing corydalis, which grows in great drifts in some of the newly cleared/replanted areas. Length 27 cm.

Unlike all our other nesting birds, the **common cuckoo** *(Cuculus canorus)* is parasitic in its breeding habits, making no nest, and depositing its eggs in the nests of other birds. The newly hatched cuckoo mounts the inner nest wall with the host bird's egg balanced on its back. When it reaches the rim, it throws the egg over the side. This action is repeated until all the eggs are removed. The most frequent hosts locally are probably the hedge accentor, wren and tree pipit. The cuckoo is recognised by blue-grey upper-parts, throat and upper breast. Under-parts are pale-grey and white barred black. On the wing it exhibits a graduated tail with white spots and tips; the long pointed wings separate it from the male sparrow-hawk, with which it is sometimes confused.

The cuckoo like a hawk in flight
With narrow pointed wings
Heaves o'er our head soon out of sight
And as he flies he sings

From the poem *Cuckoo* by JOHN CLARE

The well-known 'coocooo' song of the male has variants such as 'cooc-cooc-ooo' and the female has a water bubbling trill. Its arrival in April heralds the start of spring, but it is more often heard than seen.

A burst of colour, once dormant foxgloves in a forest clear fell area

O blithe new-comer! I have heard,
I hear thee and rejoice.
O cuckoo, shall I call thee bird,
Or but a wandering voice.

From the poem *To the Cuckoo*
by William Wordsworth

It has declined locally and nationally in recent years. Length 33 cm.

The ground-nesting **European nightjar** *(Caprimulgus europaeus)* was known locally as the 'fern owl'. This flitting ghost bird is identified by its far-carrying insect-like 'churring' call that may continue for some minutes at a time. It is usually heard at dusk or during the night. When perching it crouches lengthways on the branch almost hidden by its cryptic colouring. It is exclusively nocturnal, well adapted with long wings, large eyes and gape to catch moths, beetles and other night-flying insects whilst on the wing. These birds winter in central and southern Africa, a round trip of some 15,000 km all flown at night. In the late 1980s I caught and rang a male nightjar on Trellech Common, and the following summer I captured the same bird within 50 metres of the previous spot. This highlights the bird's remarkable navigational ability, particularly when you consider it only flies in darkness.

In 2004, as part of a national survey organised by the British Trust for Ornithology, I identified the presence of at least eight breeding pairs in the clear fell and newly planted areas. If a sitting or brooding bird feels threatened it relies on crypsis and adopts a cigar posture, with its head stretched forward with eyes closed to slits, while remaining motionless. The hunting or contact call is 'kwik–kwik', whereas the alarm note is a clearly defined harsh 'chuk' or 'chek'. Its general colour is ashy or silvery-grey, streaked with brown, chestnut and buff bars. The male has a conspicuous white spot on the outer primaries of each wing, and the two outer tail feathers on each side are tipped with white. Length 27 cm.

The visiting **tree pipit** *(Anthus trivialis)* is another ground-nester. Like a wagtail, it has a tail wagging habit, but because its tail is shorter, the action is not so conspicuous. The song is a lively, simple series of thin notes and richer trills with a slower, 'sweea, sweea, sweea' sequence near the end. It sings from a perch or, best of all, in a song flight, beginning as it reaches the top of a steep climb, and singing all the way down in a sharp, shuttlecock descent to a perch. It has brown, streaky upper-parts and paler under parts, with dark streaks on the breast. Like many other small brown birds it has a lovely subtlety when seen close up. The sexes are alike. Length 15 cm.

A tiny bird with a larger than life character is the resident **wren** *(Troglodytes troglodytes)*. It is easily recognised by its small body and short upright tail. It is hyperactive, rooting through nooks and crannies, piles of debris, and hedge bottoms in the search for insects. It is always on the move. The upper parts are warm rufous brown, boldly barred, the under-parts are lighter with bars; it has a broad creamy eye-stripe. The song is a vigorous, shrill warble that bursts out as if the singer could no longer contain it, as described by the poet W.H. Davies in his poem *Jenny Wren -*

Nightjar in a cigar-posture

Right: A tree pipit carrying food for its young

And she is known as Jenny Wren,
The smallest bird in England.
When I heard that little bird at first,
Me thought her frame would surely burst
With earnest song. Oft had I seen
Her running under leaves so green
Or in the grass when fresh and wet
As though her wings she would forget.
And, seeing this, I said to her-
"My pretty runner, you prefer
To be a thing to run unheard
Through leaves and grass, and not a bird!"
'Twas then she burst, to prove me wrong,
Into a sudden storm of song;
So very loud and earnest, I
Feared she would break her heart and die.

W.H. DAVIES

The repeated song, which lasts about five seconds, can be heard throughout the year. The alarm call is an irritable 'tic-tic-tic-tic'. It builds a domed nest, cleverly camouflaged, usually low down in the undergrowth, often appearing like a collection of dead leaves. But, as with all birds, there are exceptions. In 1997 a pair built a nest in a roll of wire netting stored in our open fronted barn, and since then the nest has been refurbished twice and used again. Maybe our local birds are becoming safety conscious! Length 9.5 cm.

Swimming Wrens

Throughout my many years spent observing birds I have never seen a wren bathing. I had always assumed they satisfied such requirements when running about in the wet foliage and undergrowth. So imagine my surprise when, one day in September, I not only saw a wren bathing but also swimming. Yes, swimming! I can honestly say I had not been drinking. In the garden we have a small rectangular stone trough that we keep

topped up with water for the birds - it is about 50 cm long, 25 cm wide, and about 15 cm deep in the centre.

I first noticed the wren splashing about at the edge of the water. In typical wren fashion the activity was conducted in a very physical manner. This went on for a good two or three minutes, at the end of which, to my great surprise, it paddled across to the other side of the trough and back again. There were then two further vigorous splashing and preening sessions, each of them followed by a paddle across the trough and back. At the end of its water sports' activity, the wren gave itself a good shake. Looking completely dry - highlighting the efficacy of the 'oil gland' - it flew off.

I have the distinct impression the wren had discovered something new and was really enjoying itself. I am waiting to witness a repeat performance.

Wren's nest in the safety of a roll of wire netting

Commonly called dunnock or hedge sparrow, the **hedge accentor** (*Prunella modularis*) is the only common member of the accentor family; a small but distinctive group mainly confined to Eurasia. It is a small bird with a rather eccentric lifestyle, always going about in small groups composed of various combinations of males or females. At first glance, it is not unlike a female house sparrow, as both have similar barring on the back, but it is its grey under-parts and streaked flanks that set it apart. In addition, the hedge accentor has a thin black beak and rusty orange-coloured eyes. The chief call note is a high pitched 'tseep' which often betrays the presence of this inconspicuous bird. The short, cheerful song is sung from a hedge top or bush, and is appreciated mainly because it is heard at the times of the year when bird song is minimal. Length 14.5 cm. Resident. It often plays host to the cuckoo as referred to by William Shakespeare.

> *The hedge-sparrow fed the cuckoo so long*
> *That it had its head bit off by its young.*

From *King Lear* by WILLIAM SHAKESPEARE

The ground hugging restless dunnock

The **whinchat** (*Saxicola rubetra*) rarely breeds here. The male is readily distinguished from the related stonechat by a white or buff eye stripe and white sides to the base of its tail. The upper-parts are brown with black markings and a light chestnut throat and breast; the female is similar but duller. Both have a white wing patch which is conspicuous in flight. The usual call uttered when approached is 'u-tick'. Length 12.5 cm. Summer visitor.

The related **common stonechat** (*Saxiola torquata*) is seldom seen here. The male is a striking bird with a black head, white on the neck and wings, a black and dark brown back, chestnut breast with pale buff under-parts. It has a habit of perching on a prominent look-out with a distinctly upright stance, often flicking its tail and uttering a harsh 'chacking' note. The female and juveniles are drabber, lacking the distinctive black head and white-patched neck. The song is a tuneful warble uttered as the male flutters in a bouncy vertical flight from his perch on the top of a bush to a height of 10-15 metres, and then dropping down again. Length 12.5 cm. Resident.

The scarce **lesser whitethroat** (*Sylvia curruca*) is one of four species of *Sylvia* warblers that visit us. It is greyer than the common whitethroat with no rufous wing feathers, and it has distinctly dark ear coverts. The throat is pure white with a tinge of buff on the breast. There are some white under-tail feathers, and the sexes are very similar. The dark coloration round the eyes gave the bird its old name of 'mountebank', a quack who wore a disguise to sell phoney medicines, so what has changed! It is a more skulking bird than the common whitethroat and, because of this, it is easily missed. The song, a simple, tuneless rattle, is uttered from a well-hidden perch. The alarm call is a sharp 'tcheck'. Length 13.5 cm.

The male **common whitethroat** (*Sylvia communis*) has an unmistakable display flight; it takes off singing, often climbing up to 30 metres high, and then immediately dives back into the undergrowth. It has a grey head with a conspicuous white throat and rufous wings; the duller female has a brown head. When disturbed it utters a scolding 'churr', a more intense alarm is expressed by a repeated hard 'tac' note. Length 14 cm.

The drab **garden warbler** (*Sylvia borin*) is a difficult bird to identify as it has no real defining visual characteristics, the upper-parts, wings and tail are a uniform olive brown, coupled with a pale eye-stripe. Garden warblers share with blackcaps and other *Sylvia* warblers the habit of making 'cock nests', which are always more frail than the one used for breeding. Its song, which is similar but mellower than that of the blackcap, is usually delivered from a hidden perch. The alarm call is a loud 'tak-tak', or a grating 'tchurr'. Length 14 cm.

The **common chiffchaff** (*Phylloscopus collybita*) is one of three species of *Phylloscopus* or leaf warblers that visit us. It is generally the first spring migrant, although it should be noted that an increasing number winter in this country. It has olive green upper-parts; the under-parts are light, lacking the yellow of the willow warbler. It announces its arrival and territorial claims by singing a repeated and monotonous 'chiff chaff, chiff chaff'. It

builds a rather untidy domed nest just above the ground, usually in the tangle where herb and shrub meet. Length 11 cm.

The **willow warbler** (*Phylloscopus trochilus*) is really only readily distinguished from its close relative by its song, a fluent series of similar wistful descending notes, and a call and alarm note, a disyllabic 'hooet'. Like the chiff-chaff it has olive green upper-parts, the under-parts are yellowish buff. It also builds a domed nest, usually on the ground, well hidden in the herbage. This is a species that has declined significantly over the last 10 years. I can remember one spring evening in 1985 finding seven nests in less than an hour, all within 200 to 300 metres of each other. Now I struggle to find one in the same area. Length 11 cm.

The resident **linnet** (*Carduelis cannabina*) is a small brown bird. The male has a brownish/grey head, red on the breast and forehead, and brown striated chestnut rump. The duller, streakier female lacks any red colouring. They often nest in loose colonies and the cheerful, twittering song is a characteristic sound wherever they appear. It was because of this attractive song that the linnet became a favourite cage-bird in the 19th century, and its widespread decline at that time was attributed to bird-catchers. On the wing they are characterised by a rather bouncy, erratic flight. This species is in decline locally and nationally. Length 13.5 cm.

The tiny active **lesser redpoll** (*Carduelis cabarnet*) can be distinguished from the linnet by a black chin. The male has a red forehead coupled with a pink breast and rump, and a striated rufous/brown back. The female lacks the pink breast and rump. They have a distinctive flight call, a rattling 'chi-chi-chi'. Over the years small flocks of up to 40 birds have regularly been seen in the autumn and spring season feeding on silver birch on the fringes of Cleddon Bog, and in a number of the mature plantations of birch. They have been suspected of breeding locally in recent years. Length 14 cm. Winter visitor and possible resident.

Willow warblers' feeding their young

The colourful **bullfinch** (*Pyrrhula pyrrhula*) is admired for its striking plumage, but disliked by some for its destructive attacks on fruit buds. The male is instantly recognisable with its black cap and rose vermilion breast, grey back and black tail. The female has a vinous brown breast and greyish-brown back. They can occur in small groups but a single pair moving along a hedge together is the more common sight. They are rather shy, usually only revealing their presence by a contact call, a soft flute-like 'pee-ew, pee-ew'. Length 14.5-16 cm. Resident.

The **yellowhammer** (*Emberiza citrinella*) is another of our resident breeding birds that is sadly in decline. The male is distinguished by a lemon yellow head (the amount of yellow varies), neck and under-parts with a chestnut rump. The white tail feathers are very conspicuous on all birds, particularly in flight. The female is duller but still has the chestnut rump. It takes up its territory very early in the year, continuously singing. Its repetitive song that sounds like '*a little bit of bread and no cheese*' either from the highest point available on the edge of its territory or quite low down close to the nest site. The call note is a grating 'twink'. Length 16.5 cm.

Male bullfinch stripping fruit buds

A colourful male yellowhammer

The seed-eating linnet on gorse

Chapter 2
Pole-stage plantation

The continuing growth of the young conifer trees will eventually deprive the competing vegetation of light, suppressing it to form a thick, dark, impenetrable jungle. At this stage the plantation will have become an inhospitable place for the majority of the birds, although species like the turtle dove, Eurasian jay, wood pigeon and song thrush will take advantage of this dark sanctuary to nest and rear their young.

In the winter, these plantations also provide a sheltered roosting place for over-wintering flocks of redwing and fieldfare, which feed in the local fields. As the developing trees continue to compete for light and space, periodic thinning and harvesting will be undertaken. This thinning lets in the beneficial sunlight again and vegetation will start to appear on the forest floor, which in turn will provide for increased insect life. Birds are quick to take advantage of these changes and move in. These are the species that can be seen.

The **Eurasian sparrowhawk** *(Accipiter nisus)* is a typical woodland hunting bird, distinguished by its short wings, necessary for dashing through the trees, and its long yellow legs and feet. The male has slate grey upper-parts, rufous cheeks, and rufous barred under-parts. The female is larger than the male and has brown upper-parts, barred below with ash-brown. They have a liking for nesting in this type of plantation, particularly larch. On the wing they utilise the 'flap-flap glide', typical of hawks. Their presence in an area is often highlighted by the use of a regular plucking post. The alarm call sounds like a rapid, harsh 'kep, kep, kep' or 'kew, kew, kew'. Length 28-38 cm. Resident.

The shy, solitary **woodcock** *(Scolopax rusticola),* nests on the plantation floor, where owing to its cryptic colouring and habit of sitting very tight, any nests are only likely to be found by accident. I know they breed here as I recently had the good fortune to see two half-grown fledglings on the edge of Cleddon Bog. It has been reported that adults will carry their small young to safety when threatened. Like most nocturnal birds they have large eyes, these are positioned on the head in a special way, providing them with good rearwards and forward vision. Its crepuscular habits and strange 'roding' flight - a slow, owl-like wing action - along well-marked territorial flight paths give this long-beaked forest wader a particular fascination. During its roding flight, it utters two distinct notes, a rather sibilant 'twisick' and a frog-like croak. It is recognised by broad dark bands across the back of the head and nape. The breast is pale buff with narrower dark bars; the back and wings have an intricate pattern of chestnut and black, intermixed with silver-grey. Length 34 cm. Resident.

The tiny **goldcrest** *(Regulus regulus)* is the smallest bird of the area, and like the coal tit is very much a bird of the coniferous woods. Its upper-parts are olive green, under-parts are dull white tinged with green, but the outstanding characteristic is a black-bordered yellow crest on its head. In the trees they are very difficult birds to locate as they flit about restlessly, mostly in the upper branches. The song, which is a very high pitched 'cedar-cedar-cedar-cedar', is one of the first calls to become

The conifer loving coal tit amongst the catkins

inaudible as the human audible frequency range contracts from middle age. Length 9 cm. Resident.

The **coal tit** *(Parus ater)* is the smallest tit of the region. It is less than half the weight of a great tit. It is recognised by a black cap and a conspicuous white patch on the nape of its neck, the upper-parts are grey, and under-parts are a dull white. When seen in silhouette, it has an unusually large head in proportion to its body and tail. More than any other of our resident tits it is more at home amongst the conifers. Its call is a fairly loud 'seeto, seeto'. Length 11.5 cm. Resident.

Along with the goldfinch the resident conifer-loving **siskin** *(Carduelis spinus)* is our smallest finch. The male can be recognised by its dark-streaked yellowish-green plumage, coupled to a black crown and chin. The female and the juveniles exhibit less yellow and are more streaked, with no black on the head. They utter a pretty twittering song - often during a 'bat-like' display flight.

The most frequent calls are 'tsuu' and 'tyszing'. In recent years this species has become a regular visitor to peanut feeders (especially red ones) in private gardens. Length 12 cm. Resident.

View through a Pole Stage Plantation

Right: A siskin on flowering larch

Chapter 3
Mature coniferous forest

Scattered throughout the district are a number of relatively small to medium size plantations of woodland. The trees vary in age from 30 to 80 years old. Each plantation contains a specific species of conifer; namely Scots pine, Corsican pine, Douglas fir or the deciduous hybrid larch and Japanese larch. The woodland floor under the canopy of the pines and firs is dominated by bracken, with some bramble and bilberry, together with a few stunted rowan, silver birch and the occasional oak.

Under the larches the woodland floor is generally more accessible. There is also bracken, bilberry and bramble, and a few stunted trees but there are also large areas of tussocky grasses. This difference is probably due to the fact that the deciduous larches lose their needles in the autumn, which lets in the sunlight and warmth throughout the winter and spring, an environment more conducive to seed germination and plant growth. These areas provide sanctuary for many types of bird.

Top of the forest food chain in Britain, the **northern goshawk** *(Accipiter gentilis)* was thought to have become extinct in the 19th century, but became a regular breeder again from the early 1960s. It is thought the present population is derived from escapees from falconers. The Wye Valley and the Forest of Dean have one of the healthiest populations of these birds. A rather secretive bird, the northern goshawk is best described as an outsize sparrowhawk and is readily distinguished from a buzzard, which is similar in size, by its shorter wings and longer tail. The call is a shrill 'ca-ca-ca-ca'or 'qek-qek-qek', the female utters a screaming 'hi-aa, hi-aa'. Length 48-61 cm. Resident.

The **common buzzard** *(Buteo buteo)* is the most common resident raptor of the district. These birds can often be seen on open ground searching for earthworms. I have seen as many as 12 buzzards in the same field looking for worms, but rabbits also form a very important part of their diet. Their dependence on rabbits was one of the main contributory factors in the decline of the buzzard population at the height of the myxomatosis epidemic in 1954, which nearly wiped out the rabbit population. The buzzard population has since fully recovered from this setback. They catch mostly half-grown rabbits weighing between 250 and 500 grams. After detecting them from a favourite perch, they make an approach with a gentle glide before swooping on their prey. On the wing, buzzards appear as large, short-necked, broad-winged and rather short-tailed birds. They have a soaring flight, on raised, often-crooked wings, occasionally hovering. The colour of their plumage varies from dark to pale brown. The usual call is a plaintive mewing; the warning call is a shrill yelp. Length 51-56 cm.

The **tawny owl** *(Strix aluco)* is the owl most often seen here. It is often detected in daytime hunched up in its tree roost and being mobbed by other birds. These owls can be fearless in defence of their young, and people have been attacked and injured by them. In Wales in 1937 the famous bird photographer Eric Hosking lost his left eye in such an incident. It is now recommended that anyone approaching tawny owls with young should wear some form of eye protection.

A young tawny owl

A picture of concentration, a young buzzard

do fall to the ground they just climb the nearest tree. The adult is always nearby watching. It has rich chestnut brown mottled upper-parts; the under-parts are buff with dark streaks. It is possibly known as the 'staring owl' from Shakespeare.

When icicles hang by the wall
And Dick the shepherd blows his nail.
When Tom bears logs into the hall
And milk comes frozen home in pail.
When blood is nipped and ways are foul
Then nightly sings the staring owl tu-whit,
tu-whoo,
A merry note while greasy Joan doth keel the pot.

From *Love's Labour's Lost*
by WILLIAM SHAKESPEARE

This rendering of its call is adequate, but the note is more of a prolonged 'hou'. The nocturnal hooting and 'ke-wick' calls make location of the breeding territory easy. Length 38 cm. Resident.

The resident **great spotted woodpecker** *(Dendrocopos major)* is a black and white bird with a prominent white patch on each wing and red under-tail coverts. The male has a red nape. The flight is conspicuously bounding, its wings being folded against the body at the bottom of each bound. Its nest is usually made in a decaying tree trunk, either in deciduous or coniferous woods.

These woodpeckers regularly attack nest-boxes, hewing them open and eating the eggs or young. The call note is a sharp 'kik', usually uttered singly. The bird may be heard 'drumming' in the breeding season.

This drumming sound is generated by striking a selected branch or tree trunk with its beak. During this action both mandibles of its beak are held together by a locking device to stop them opening. The force generated is of such intensity that if it were transmitted directly to the brain the bird would be knocked unconscious. The reason this does not happen is because the brain is

A few years ago I had a minor confrontation with a tawny owl when I found a downy-covered owlet on the ground in a local wood. Thinking it was at risk, I picked it up and placed it on a branch of a nearby tree. As I turned to walk away, I was struck a violent blow on the back of my head, which knocked me to the ground. I looked up just in time, to see the hitherto unspotted adult flying into the tree near to the owlet, so be warned!

The young ones leave the nest long before they are able to fly, but they are very good at climbing, so if they sited above the centre line, of its beak, and the associated muscles at the base of the beak absorb and cushion the shock. Length 23 cm. Resident.

The Ultimate Deterrent?

One spring I was witness to a struggle between a great spotted woodpecker and a nuthatch for the use of an old woodpecker hole as a nest site. The hole was in a rotting Scots pine close to the woodland edge. I first noticed the woodpecker inspecting the hole inside and out, and it also spent quite a long time clinging motionless to the tree very close to it.

My immediate thought was that it intended to re-use the site. However, a couple of days later I was surprised to see a nuthatch emerge from the hole. It was apparent that it had taken over, and had started to reduce the size of the entrance hole by introducing mud. The woodpecker was nowhere to be seen, so I assumed it had abandoned the plan.

This was not the case, for later in the day I saw the great spotted woodpecker come out of the hole and remain clinging to the tree, while carrying out another external inspection. Throughout this period the nuthatch was nearby, constantly 'alarm calling'. The next day the nuthatch was back in charge, and once again was working away carrying mud to reduce the size of the hole. There was no sign of the woodpecker.

It was a few days before I went back to the tree. This time the great spotted woodpecker was looking out from the hole, and some of the mud had been removed from the entrance. Once again the nuthatch was protesting nearby. This cycle of events was repeated a number of times over the next few days with neither bird apparently prepared to give way.

Then there was a change. As I approached the wood across the fields I noticed that the nuthatch was pecking at and collecting some pieces of rain-soaked fox droppings, which it carried to the nest site and proceeded to daub around the entrance hole. It then flew on to the trunk of an adjacent pine tree and started to strip off small pieces of bark. It carried these strips back to the nest site, and proceeded to stick them on to the fox droppings and mud around the nest entrance. In the past I had seen a nuthatch use material from a cow pat to reduce the size of an entrance hole, but this combination was much more imaginative. It continued applying this mixture for some considerable time, during which there was no sign of the woodpecker. It occurred to me, as I stood there watching, that perhaps I should forward these observations to the Building Research Centre. Could this amalgam provide the basis for a revolutionary new type of chip-board!

For whatever reason the woodpecker never returned. Unfortunately the story does not have a happy ending, for the resultant nuthatch brood failed due to the cold damp spring weather, and the associated shortages of natural food.

Great spotted woodpecker with food for its young

Mirror, Mirror in the Pool

Throughout one recent winter and early spring, a pair of great spotted woodpeckers had fed regularly at a peanut feeder in the garden. About the end of June I was interested to see that the female had brought two of her youngsters into the garden with her. She left them perched in a nearby tree, and flew to and from the supply of nuts, feeding them. After she had finished, she flew to the nearby bird-bath for a drink and then returned to the tree. Immediately, one of the youngsters flew down to the bath 'to have a go at this drinking lark'. To my amusement, as it was leaning forward to drink, it jumped up into the air uttering a raucous alarm and landed on the ground a few metres away. It had obviously been frightened by its own reflection, which it had not seen before. After a short period of careful watching, it recovered its composure and flew back for a drink, with no more alarms.

The **Eurasian treecreeper** (*Certhia familiaris*) is the only small brown bird of the district with a decurved beak. The forked tail is graduated with stiff pointed feathers and white under-parts. Its presence is more often detected by ear than by eye, as it creeps mouse-like up tree trunks looking for insects in a series of spasmodic jerks, unhurried, but always on the move. It always starts at the base of the tree and spirals upwards. The nest is usually established behind loose bark or ivy. The call note is a rather prolonged high-pitched 'tsee, tsee, tsee'. Length 12.5 cm. Resident.

The **common redstart** (*Phoenicurus phoenicurus*) is a summer visitor to Britain, with its main winter quarters in West Africa. The striking male has a white forehead, the sides of the face and throat are black, the mantle and back are slate grey, chestnut breast, the under-parts are pale buff and white, and the rump and tail are a fiery chestnut, which gives the bird its name. The female has brownish upper-parts, the under-parts are paler, and the flanks are a pale rufous buff. The song is a rather pleasant, varied warble, similar at times to the chaffinch and the pied flycatcher. The main calls are an 'hwee-ticc-ticc' and a willow warbler-like 'hooet'; the alarm call is a sharp 'tic'. The nest is built in a hole in a tree, a tree stump, a dry wall, or occasionally in a hole in the ground. Length 14 cm.

Treecreeper, an unusual nest site under a building facia board

Charades

In late April and early May a pair of redstarts came regularly into the garden to bathe in and drink from a small puddle in the drive, which subsequently dried out during the early spell of hot weather. One day I was surprised to see the male redstart visit the site where the puddle used to be and go through the apparent routine of drinking and bathing, even though there was no water. It wasn't dusty either, so there was no suggestion of possible dust bathing.

I looked around for the audience - no sign - they had obviously guessed wrong anyway, as he went

Right: A redstart among the foxgloves in a clear fell area

through the routine a few more times before finally flying off, presumably to sulk, or visit his 'shrink'! I shouted after him, 'I know what you were doing, my turn now'. No, I am only joking. I view this as a classic example of instinctive behaviour triggered by association.

The **common crossbill** *(Loxia curvirostra)* is notable for its crossed, hooked bill, which is specially adapted to extract seeds from cones on conifers. Their presence locally as a breeding or visiting species is erratic. They fly in from Europe in search of food, often in large numbers. These influxes are called irruptions. Once they identify a good feeding area they will probably stay and breed - and then move on when the food source has been stripped. The adult male is crimson, with a touch of orange, with dark brown wings and tail. The female is green with a hint of yellow, and a dark tail. Occasionally you see birds with two narrow white wing bars; it is possible that these are hybrids, having interbred with the two-barred crossbill, itself a rare visitor to Britain. Its call note, frequently uttered on the wing, is a metallic 'chip-chip'. Length 16.5 cm. Resident.

A male crossbill showing its powerful cross bill and strong climbing feet

View of mature coniferous woodland showing a wind blown tree

Right: A pair of crossbills drinking, the male exhibiting white wing bars

Chapter 4
Mature mixed and broad-leaved woodland

These areas of woodland are generally dominated by a mixture of oak and beech mixed in with European larch and Douglas fir, together with the occasional rowan, silver birch, Spanish chestnut and wild cherry. Some of these may have grown from seeds brought in by birds.

Bargain Wood and Creigiau Wood near Whitestone are some of the oldest examples of this type of woodland, parts of which date back to the middle and latter parts of the 19th century. The central part of Bargain Wood, which is entirely oak and beech, was planted in 1900. In the spring an early morning walk there is truly inspirational, with 'Mother Nature in all her glory'. You are presented with the wonderful sight of fresh, light green, translucent beech leaves, highlighted by shafts of filtered sunlight and a profusion of bluebells on the woodland floor. All this coupled with a dawn chorus, what more could one wish for? These areas of woodland provide a home for a variety of birds:

The **green woodpecker** *(Picus viridis)* is readily distinguished from all the other birds by its combination of green plumage, a yellow-green rump that is conspicuous in flight, and its red head. The call is, as author and naturalist the Revd Gilbert White phrased it, *'a sort of loud and hearty laugh'* - an ancient rendering of which gave the bird one of its popular names, the 'yaffle'. The species also 'drums', but less so than the spotted forms. Unlike our other native woodpeckers, it spends a lot of time feeding on the ground, especially on anthills. Length 32 cm. Resident.

The sparrow-sized **lesser spotted woodpecker** *(Dendrocopus minor)* is the smallest British woodpecker. Its black and white barred appearance is distinctive and fully explains the species' former name of barred woodpecker. It is scarce locally and, because they spend much of their time high amongst the smaller branches of trees, they can easily be overlooked. The call notes are a rather weak 'pee-pee-pee-pee-pee' and a weak sibilant 'tchik'. Despite its size it drums loudly and extremely fast, 12 to 15 blows per second, compared with the great spotted woodpecker, which drums at eight to ten blows per second. Length 14.5 cm. Resident.

The **wood warbler** *(Phylloscopus sibilatrix)* is the largest of our visiting leaf warblers. It is greener than the other related warblers, with a yellowish breast, white under-parts and a distinct yellow eye-stripe. The song that readily identifies it is a long shivering trill uttered whilst vibrating its wings and tail, or sometimes in flight between perches. The song is often punctuated with a plaintive, piping 'peu, peu, peu'. Length 12.5 cm.

The **pied flycatcher** *(Ficedula hypoleuca)* is a summer visitor. The male is strikingly black and white, while the female is plain brown with some white on the wings and tail. Despite its name, it feeds to a large extent on insects found on foliage, and caterpillars are a major food source. It is rather scarce here, and its presence as a breeding bird is totally dependent on the availability of nesting holes. It takes very readily to nest-boxes. Primarily a bird of the broad-leaved woodland, particularly sessile oak, it will adapt to coniferous woods if nest sites are available. Its song delivered from a perch

Wood warbler feeding young

Male green woodpecker visiting nest site

The closely related **willow tit** (*Parus montanus*) is also relatively scarce. It was only identified as a new species in 1900, and is difficult to distinguish from the marsh tit. Both the willow tit, which is equally at home in the coniferous woodland and the marsh tit tend to favour the scrubby areas of the woodland. The willow tit has a sooty black crown, nape and chin, pale cheeks and under-parts. Unlike the marsh tit, it has an obscure lighter patch on its secondaries. The typical call note is a grating, nasal 'tchay' sometimes preceded by 'chick'. It is the only resident tit that excavates its own nest hole. Length 11.5 cm.

Willow tit prospecting for food

has been aptly rendered as *'tree, tree, tree, once more I come to thee'*. Length 13 cm.

The **marsh tit** (*Parus palustris*) has a black crown, nape and chin, pale cheeks and under-parts. The adult bird has a glossy black crown and no pale patch on its wing; these are the two main visual differences from the closely related willow tit. Typical call note is 'pitchuu', often followed by a harsh 'tchay', less grating than the willow tit. This species is also rather scarce here. Length 11.5 cm. Resident.

The highly acrobatic **blue tit** (*Parus caeruleus*) specialises in feeding at the extreme ends of branches, and is the only tit of the area that appears mainly blue and yellow; the blue on the head is particularly distinctive. The most typical call is a rather scolding 'tsee-tsee-tsee-tit'. Next to the robin, it must be the best loved of the birds that visit our gardens. Length 11.5 cm. Resident.

The aptly named **great tit** *(Parus major)* is our largest resident tit and is easily recognised by a black and white head coupled with a black bib running down the centre of its yellow under-parts. It has an extensive vocabulary, which includes a distinctive 'teechah, teechah', a welcome sign that spring is just around the corner. It is recorded as having well over 50 different calls. So if you hear a small bird calling and cannot recognise the call, there is a good chance it's a great tit. Length 14 cm.

The small, short-tailed, tree-climbing **European nuthatch** *(sitta europaea)* is distinguished by blue-grey upper-parts, whitish throat, rufous-buff under-parts and a pronounced black eye-stripe. It is the only bird that habitually descends trees head downward with a jerky gait. They are hole nesters and where the entrance hole is too large, admitting a larger species, they will reduce it to their required size by lining the inner circumference with mud. In the absence of mud, I have known them use cow manure; birds are always adaptable opportunists. Its presence may be revealed by loud tapping noises, made as the bird hammers nuts open. Its usual calls are a loud piping 'pee, pee, pee', ringing 'chwit-chwit' or a sibilant long-tailed tit like 'tsirrup'. Length 14 cm. Resident.

The shy and scarce **hawfinch** *(Coccothraustes coccothraustes)* is difficult to observe and is most likely to be seen in the autumn feeding on beech mast in Manor Wood. It is the largest of our finches and can be recognised by its mainly chestnut plumage, with black wing tips and throat, striking white wing-bar and white border to the tail. But the most striking characteristic is its outsize bill; this is grey-blue in the summer and yellow in the winter. Its large pyramidal beak can exert pressures of over $97N/cm^2$ enabling it to extract the kernels of damsons and sloes. The most frequent call notes are a sharp 'zick' and a high- pitched sibilant 'tsip'. Length 18 cm. Resident.

Great tit enjoying the morning sunshine amongst the catkins

Nuthatch in characteristic head down attitude

Nest Robbers

Those skinheads of the avian world the magpies and the jays have again wreaked havoc on the small nesting birds in our garden. From my observations I would say that the magpie, which is the dominant species of the two, was the chief executioner. The garden is bordered by woods on three sides and by farmland on the other, hence the presence of both species. Out of 15 nests, 10 were predated. The species that suffered were blackbird, wren, chaffinch, bullfinch, greenfinch (three nests), goldfinch, hedge accentor and goldcrest. Most of the losses seemed to occur early in the morning when the offenders, and offended, were feeding young. My observation has shown that in general both species seem to find the nests by what appears to be systematic searching of the hedgerows and bushes, although in the case of the jay (a more secretive bird), a number of the nests were probably found by watching.

Many letters and articles have been written on the increase of magpies and their possible effect on the small bird population. I think the jury is still out on the subject, with the public in general saying they are 'guilty' and the experts saying 'not guilty'. The conclusion may be that their overall effect nationwide is minimal, but I have no doubt that in discrete areas the damage they inflict is significant.

On the subject of jays their population in the Trellech Common and Beacon Hill area has increased significantly over the last few years, particularly in the young conifer plantations. I believe this has played a part in the decrease in this habitat of such species as linnet, yellowhammer, tree pipit, willow warbler and whitethroat; although I do accept that there are many contributory factors.

The **Eurasian jay** *(Garrulus glandarius)* has been called '*the British bird of paradise*' by the ornithologist and author W. H. Hudson. It is distinguished by its pink-fawn back, pale brownish under-parts coupled to a patch of white, blue and black on the wings and a conspicuous white rump and black tail. The black and white feathers on the crown can be erected to form a crest. Its flight is rather weak and undulating, and when on the ground it hops in a rather ungainly fashion. The most identifiable call is a harsh scolding screech 'skaaak, skaaak'. It is equally at home in deciduous or coniferous woods. Length 34 cm. Resident.

Right: A foraging jay

Chapter 5
On the woodland's edge

This is where the roadside verge or farmland meets the woodland. As a result of the greater ingress of sunlight and associated warmth, the 10 to 15 metres of woodland fringe may encompass a hedge, low bank or both, providing a mixture of mature trees, together with a tangle of elder, holly, hawthorn, sometimes gorse, and bramble, nettles and other herbage. As ecologists inform us, the edge between two different habitats contains the richest variety of species. Such a mixture provides the environment for a variety of insect life that will help support the following birds:

The **robin** (*Erithacus rubecula*). If there is a British national bird it must be the robin, which hardly needs any description, and is aptly described by William Wordsworth.

> *Art thou the bird, whom man loves best,*
> *The pious bird with the scarlet breast,*
> *Our little English robin;*
> *The bird that comes about our doors*
> *When autumn winds are sobbing?*
> *The bird who by some name or other*
> *All men who know thee call their brother?*

The Robin by WILLIAM WORDSWORTH

The robin's throat and breast are orange-red margined with blue-grey, light under-parts; the upper-parts are olive brown. One associates the pleasant warbling song of the robin with autumn and winter. There is in it a touch of quiet melancholy, reminiscent of the drifting fall of autumn leaves. The alarm call is a sharp 'tic, tic'. Length 14 cm. Resident.

The male **blackbird** (*Turdus merula*) is the only jet-black bird of the area that has a bright orange-yellow beak and a yellow eye-ring. The female is umber brown, with a brownish bill and indistinct streaks on a lighter breast. Immature birds are similar to the female; the bill in the male is black until the second year. The song is not composed of repeated phrases like the song thrush but is a series of short warbles, with varied notes, the best being mellow flute-like sounds unsurpassed by any bird. The ornithologist W.H. Hudson wrote:

> *The charm is chiefly due to the intrinsic beauty of the sound: it is fluty and has that quality of the flute suggestive of the human voice, the voice in the case of the blackbird of an exquisitely pure and beautiful contralto. The effect is greatly increased by the manner in which the notes are emitted - trolled out leisurely, as if by a being at peace and supremely happy.*

The alarm call is a rapid 'tchuck-tchuck-tchuck-tchuck'. Length 25 cm. Resident.

The **song thrush** (*Turdus philomelos*) is recognised by its olive brown back and dark spots on a pale breast. Slightly warmer brown under-parts and the lack of white in the tail distinguish it from the larger mistle thrush. Its song, loud and clear and sometimes mimetic can be heard throughout most of the year; it can be told from other thrush songs as it has a propensity to repeat each note.

An attentive male blackbird feeding its young

The 'Ecstasy and Agony'

One morning in late July I was taking the dog for her regular early morning walk when she discovered a partly fledged song thrush nestling in the grass on the edge of a young conifer plantation. Judging from its size and development it was less than a week old. A quick search failed to find a nest, and, as the adults were alarming close by, I placed the nestling under the canopy of a small sitka spruce, and continued my walk. That evening I repeated the walk with the dog, but never thought to check if the nestling was still where I had placed it.

On arriving home it was nearly dark, and it had just started to rain. As was so often the case the dog failed to return with me, having discovered too many interesting smells to investigate. I whistled and shouted a couple of times, but there was no response so I went indoors. After about 10 minutes I looked out of the back window to see if she had returned.

Sure enough she was on the lawn and, judging by her behaviour, not alone. I went outside and found her standing over the nestling she had discovered earlier in the day. This meant she had carried it about 400 metres from where we had seen it that morning. My dog was a dobermann, so I was surprised to find that the nestling was still alive. I thought that if I took the nestling back in the dark to where I had first seen it, its chances of survival were slim, so the household decision was that we should try and rear it. It was very bedraggled, and obviously very hungry, so the first task was to go into the garden and dig up some worms. While I 'ploughed' the vegetable plot to find a dozen worms, my wife found an artificial beak, old eyebrow tweezers tucked away in her make-up bag, so feeding began. This turned out to be very simple, for the nestling was ravenous, and didn't need any encouragement. In no time it had consumed eight worms, whereupon it promptly went to sleep - without even needing a bedtime story!

So far, so good. The next step was to find it a temporary home. We found a cardboard box, covered the bottom with paper and placed an artificial nest fabricated from newspaper inside. About 30 minutes had elapsed since the initial feed and already it was chirping for more. So Oliver seemed an appropriate name. He seemed happy enough with it, and immediately ate another four worms and went to sleep again. We placed him in the nest and closed the box for the night.

In the morning we woke up wondering if Ollie had survived the night. Our fears were unwarranted, for as soon as he heard us he started to 'cheep'. When I lifted the box lid, he opened his beak and flapped his wings. I fed him five more worms, and then it was wellingtons on and out into the garden to find more. Ollie was fed roughly every 30 minutes, 12 hours a day for the next five days, eating four or five worms at every sitting.

We kept him in the house, cleaning out his box each day. We were very impressed with his toilet habits, for he always left his droppings on the side of his nest ready for removal. Despite his immense appetite his progress was very slow. Although by now at least 12 days old he could not stand up properly, and his feather development was very poor. I began to think he was probably a runt, and had become isolated when his siblings left the nest.

We decided to put him outside in the car-port during the day so he could re-acquaint himself with the real world. He never moved far but showed he was very adept at finding the sunny places, so when he wasn't eating, he was dozing in the sun, occasionally finding some insects to peck at. We also tried feeding him some small pieces of cheese, thinking that a bit of extra calcium might aid his development. Although he seemed happy to eat one or two pieces at every feeding session, that was his limit, then he would flick any further pieces away and beg for more worms.

By now he had acquired the art of breaking the large worms into small pieces before eating them. This was achieved by giving the worm a sharp peck, which broke the skin. He then gave the worm a sharp flick, severing it at the damaged point. To add further variety to his diet we introduced him to bilberries, but, as with the cheese, he was very selective about how many he ate.

Over the next couple of days he seemed to gain in strength, with the result that when I went to feed him he would hop towards me in anticipation. By now his feathers were developing well, although he still had some bald patches around his neck and on his underside.

Although he was outside during the day, we still kept him indoors inside his box at nights, but the time came when his plumage had improved sufficiently for that to change. Before moving his box out of doors I installed a perch, thinking its use would satisfy his basic perching habits. It would also help to develop the toes on his left foot which appeared very weak and tended to curl under. I also introduced him to something that forms a very important part of his natural diet: slugs.

The first offering was a small common netted slug about 35 mm long - this was closely inspected, pecked at, turned over several times, and then finally eaten. This action was then followed by vigorous wiping of his beak on the ground to remove the sticky mucous. Subsequent offerings were treated with the same circumspection and routine, but the removal of the sticky mucous from his beak was obviously causing him some problems.

After a couple of days - and to my amazement - he solved the problem. On being offered a slug his first action now was to wipe it vigorously on the ground removing a lot of the mucous before consuming it. A perfect example of instinctive behaviour. It had to be, for there was no parent bird to show him. Although he was by now finding the occasional worm himself I was still feeding him upwards of 40 worms and slugs daily. Assuming his appetite was normal, the question I kept asking myself was how do the parent birds manage to feed four or five nestlings, particularly during a dry spell? I was certainly finding it difficult to keep him satisfied.

A further example of his instinctive behaviour showed itself when I was feeding him. He always like to stand in my shadow, and when a large bird like a magpie or buzzard flew overhead he used to freeze, with his beak pointing to the sky and his little black beady eyes locked on to his potential enemy. Throughout the feeding sessions he used to keep up a constant twittering and when replete he would hop away into a shady place.

Ollie had now been with us for about two weeks. Although his feather growth appeared slow he was gaining in strength, and the toes on his left foot now appeared to be nearly normal. Although I was still putting him in his box at night he was becoming more adventurous in his travels. He was also capable of flying five to 10 metres, but was still very dependent on us for food. He had established that whenever we went out to feed him we would always use the back door of the house, so when he was hungry he would come to the door and call until he elicited a response from us. By the end of the third week his feathers, particularly his tail feathers, had grown, so, now complete with his operational rudder, he could fly for 20 to 30 metres.

About this time I thought he should have a bath and again I was curious to know how he would react. I placed some water in an inverted dustbin lid, placed it in the sun and stood him in it. Within seconds he had squatted down and was having the time of his life, splashing water everywhere. After about a minute he hopped out, shook himself and then found a sunny spot close to the sanctuary of some bushes, whereupon he settled down to bask and give his feathers a thorough preening. Once again this was a perfect example of instinctive behaviour, even to the extent of selecting a safe site to bask.

By now he was becoming much more independent, but if I could not find him all I had to do was to shout 'Ollie' and he would usually arrive via a combination of flying and hopping. Like all thrushes he was good at hopping, and when he was in full flow the bouncy movement was reminiscent of a kangaroo. One evening in the fourth week he failed to respond to my calls, and I was starting to think the worst when I heard him calling from an apple tree. As far as I know this was his first arboreal adventure, and his first attempt to roost away from his box. After I had caught him and put him in his box, I could tell from the movements within, that he was restless. It was becoming apparent that the call of the wild was growing stronger so we decided that if the weather the following evening was fine we would leave him out overnight. As luck would have it the next evening was fine, so we fed him some worms at about 8 o'clock, and then left him to his own devices.

The following morning I stepped outside wondering whether we would ever see Ollie again, but before I had taken a dozen steps I heard his 'chortling' call and a sound of whirring wings and before I could turn round he had alighted on my shoulder. To me this was a moment of pure magic; he seemed almost as pleased to see me as I was to see him. Over the next few days as he continued to become more self sufficient, the intervals between feeding became longer and the amounts eaten smaller. However, when I went to the vegetable garden to dig up the potatoes for dinner, he usually followed me there, and would take advantage, of any worms or slugs that were exposed. Some of the worms could be up to 15 cm long and as thick as one's finger but they were all consumed without any problem.

Despite his new self-reliance he would always respond to his name, sometimes flying to me, and other times just calling out. I usually found him foraging amongst the leaves in the hedge bottom or under the garden shrubs. We had now looked after him for nearly six weeks, and although on the small size he was fully feathered and flying well. It was this lack of size that convinced me that he must have been a runt.

The sixth week started with a major panic when my wife saw a sparrow-hawk sweep through the garden. We both dashed outside expecting to see a pile of feathers, but all was well. At this stage all direct feeding had stopped, although when I was working in the garden he would still appear and take advantage of any offerings. He was totally fearless, avoiding my feet and the moving garden tools at the last split second. He always made certain he was at the focal point of any soil disturbance, so that he could snap up any tasty morsels that might be on offer, all the time keeping up a non-stop twittering as though holding a conversation.

We were starting to think he would be around for years, as song thrushes have been recorded as living in the wild up to the age of 14 years. Alas, this was not to be. One day after a gardening session he flew into the kitchen window and broke his neck. The household was devastated; we had all become very attached to this small bird whose needs, particularly during the first three weeks, had dictated our daily routine. Our overriding memories, though, will be of his instinctive behaviour, his ability to learn, and most of all his complete trust in us. The thrill of having a wild animal responding to one's call far exceeds any similar response from a domestic pet.

A male greenfinch amongst blackthorn blossom

The long-winged, strong-bodied **greenfinch** (*Carduelis chloris*) is unmistakable, for the male has bright yellow wing patches and rump whereas the female is generally duller. The song is a medley of twittering sounds, often delivered in a bat-like circular flight, a strong nasal 'dzhwee' is also often uttered in the breeding season. Length 14.5 cm. Resident.

The summer-visiting **blackcap** (*Sylvia atricapilla*) is relatively easy to identify. The adult male has a distinctive black cap; the nape and breast are grey. The female has a brown cap and there is a touch of brown on an otherwise grey breast. The song of the blackcap is rich and melodious, on occasions rivalling that of the blackbird or nightingale, but it can easily be confused with that of the garden warbler, which is lower pitched, and of a longer duration. Length 14 cm.

The **spotted flycatcher** (*Muscicapa striata*) is one of the last of our summer migrants to reach us, often not seen before mid-May. It is a sparrow-sized grey-brown bird with dark streaks on the head and breast, the underparts are lighter, and the sexes are alike. It is an effortless flyer, and its skilled aerobatics as it sallies out from its favourite perch to catch insects on the wing, returning to the same perch, mark it out as our only true flycatcher. The usual call is a long thin robin-like 'tzeee'. When alarmed it utters a 'check' or 'chick'. This is another bird whose numbers are declining alarmingly, both locally and nationally. Length 14 cm.

Confused Flycatchers

One summer a pair of spotted flycatchers built a nest in our barn on a ledge at the interface between a first floor joist and the supporting cross beam, and on completion they built a second nest in the adjacent identical niche. No sooner had they completed this nest than they started to build a third one. Where, I wondered, would this end? Was this the first sign of private enterprise in the avian world? Perhaps they are going to rent out the nests, for so many flies a day? Houseflies, of course!

This nest building took place over a period of about 10 days. Looking in again later, expecting to find a fourth nest under construction, I was relieved to find a bird sitting on the first nest. A couple of days later there was a bird on the second nest. My immediate thought was, 'I was right, they have set up in business and the first tenant has moved in!' On closer inspection I saw there were two eggs in each of the first two nests, but the third was empty. Observing the nests later in the day, I saw a bird was sitting on nest one again. Knowing that spotted flycatchers are solitary nesters and that a pair can share the incubation, I thought, 'I know what has happened, they have had a row and have decided to live apart and bring up two youngsters each!' Then reality set in. This was silly. But I was concerned that as the pair alternated between nests it was extremely likely both pairs of eggs would fail through lack of sustained warmth so I placed all four eggs in nest one. Next time I looked, a bird was sitting on this nest, and I am pleased to report four young were successfully reared.

Twelve months later a pair of spotted flycatchers again nested successfully in the apex of the barn. Then I noticed that they were starting to build in the same place as the previous summer, completing one nest and then moving on to the adjacent niche to build the second. I thought, 'I have seen all this before' but this time there was a further twist in that they built a double nest. There were no further surprises and four eggs were laid in one nest of the double, and a healthy brood was reared,

This nest building by the spotted flycatchers provides a perfect example of the problems posed to birds when presented with a series of identical compartments or niches. They have not yet adapted to cope with situations which do not occur naturally in the wild; consequently when they select one niche to nest in they become confused and are likely to build a number of nests or part nests in adjacent identical niches. 'Multiple nest building' and 'split clutch laying' has been recorded for a number of species, notably dippers, grey wagtails and blackbirds, which often nest below bridges where there may be a series of similar ledges.

Spotted flycatcher and expectant young

The aptly named **long-tailed tit** *(Aegithalos caudatus)* is a small black, white and pink bird whose tail accounts for more than half its total length. It is renowned for its domed nest that is built mainly of mosses, hair and cobwebs, camouflaged with lichens and lined with feathers - up to 2,000 in number; think of all those journeys to collect them! Gorse is a favoured nest site. These tits are often seen in groups flying from tree to tree following each other in a string formation; the flight is weak and undulating. The usual call note heard as the birds wander in these small flocks is a cheerful 'tzee, tzee, tzee' followed at times by 'tsirrip, tsirrip'. Length 14 cm. Resident.

The **chaffinch** *(Fringilla coelebs)* is the commonest finch we have, although even its numbers have decreased in recent years. The male has a slate blue crown and nape, a chestnut brown mantle, white shoulder patch, greenish rump, sienna brown throat and breast; the female is much duller. Its commonest call note is a persistent 'pink, pink' similar to a great tit, and it has an insistent warning 'wheet, wheet'. Winter flocks feed in more open country, often with other finches. Length 15 cm. Resident.

The **brambling** *(Fringilla montifringilla)* is an unpredictable winter visitor, with numbers varying yearly. The best field mark is a white rump, very conspicuous when the bird is flying away, and an orange-buff breast and shoulders. The male has a black head and mantle in the breeding season; otherwise it is buffish like the female and juveniles. The usual call note is a rather harsh ' tsweek'. These birds are often seen in flocks with chaffinches. Length 14.5 cm.

Our largest thrush, the **mistle thrush** *(Turdus viscivorus)* is a pale greyish colour with larger breast spots than the song thrush. Its country name of 'stormcock' is highly suitable as it sings loudly from a high perch in all weathers, particularly in the spring. The name mistle thrush is no less apt, as it does specialise in eating mistletoe berries in the winter when available. The alarm note is a harsh scolding 'churr'. It has a characteristic flight shared with the fieldfare, the wings being closed at regular intervals without producing a markedly undulating flight. Length 27 cm. Resident.

Winter visiting male brambling

Chapter 6
On field and farm

Farms are places where crops are grown, either for direct consumption by people or livestock or for processing by machinery into food or raw material. Consequently farmland is generally a mixture of grazing and arable land. Regardless of the type of farm, the farmer needs to improve his farm's productivity, its shelter in terms of buildings and also to establish a forward-looking plan. In pursuit of this, he can have a preserving, improving or destructive impact on bird habitats.

Over the last decade, more arable farming has been introduced into this area of Wales where once livestock farming was predominant. Financial issues, resulting from the European Union's common agricultural policy and its associated enforced policy changes, in what is an ever increasingly materialistic 'money mad' political world, have driven these changes. It is possible to observe the following birds in or over the farmland of the district:

The resident **grey heron** *(Ardea cinera)* is readily recognised by its large size, long yellow beak, long legs, and mainly grey plumage with a white head and neck, and a black crest. When standing gaunt and motionless in the shadows a heron can be mistaken for a post or dead branch, and even when walking its movements are so slow and stealthy it can easily be overlooked. The flight is slow and majestic, the legs trail and the long neck is drawn in, producing a conspicuous bulge. Herons nest in colonies, building large nests of sticks, usually high in trees. The usual call is a harsh 'kraaank'; at the nest site they produce a castanet-like beak snapping. They do not nest around Trellech, but are often seen and occasionally visit local garden ponds to steal the fish. Length 90 cm.

The ubiquitous **mallard** *(Anas platyrhynchos)* is our largest dabbling duck and is the origin of all our farmyard ducks. It is very adaptable, accepting almost any kind of waterside habitat. The drake is recognised by the glossy green head and neck, a white ring around the neck, and up-curled tail feathers. The back and under-parts are grey; the breast is a dark purple brown. The overall colour is unmatched by any other water bird. The duck is dark brown and lacks the curled-up tail feathers. Mallard nest sites vary greatly and are often far from water. Some years ago, I found a nest amongst newly planted conifers on Beacon Hill at least 2 km from any significant water. Unusual sites include flower boxes, static water tanks and holes in trees. Length 58 cm. Resident.

Like all falcons, the **common kestrel** *(Falco tinnunculus)* has long pointed wings, and when seen from certain angles the tail looks exceptionally long. It is probably best known for its hovering:

> *I caught this morning morning's minion, kingdom*
> *of daylight's dauphin, dapple-dawn-drawn Falcon,*
> *in his riding*
> *Of the rolling level underneath him steady air,*
> *and striding*
> *High there, how he rung upon the rein of a*
> *wimpling wing*
> *In his ecstasy! Then off, off forth on swing,*
> *As a skate's heel sweeps smooth on a bow-bend:*
> *the hurl and gliding*

Rebuffed the big wind. My heart in hiding
Stirred for a bird, - the achieve of,
the mastery of the thing!

From the poem *The Windhover*
by GERARD MANLEY HOPKINS

The male has a blue-grey head, nape and tail, the latter having a white edged tip and a broad black sub-terminal bar. Its back is chestnut with black spots, the under-parts are buff, streaked and spotted with black. The female does not have the blue-grey colouring. The call is a loud, clear 'kee-kee-kee'. This is another species that has declined locally over the last decade. Length 34 cm. Resident.

The summer-visiting **hobby** *(Falco subbuteo)* is a trans-Saharan migrant and a late spring arrival to Britain. It is present on its breeding territory for only a short time, with most eggs being laid in mid-June. Truly mercurial flyers, these birds are overhead one moment and distant specks the next. They have long scythe-like wings and, at a distance, the silhouette resembles a large swift. They feed largely on small birds taken on the wing, such as swifts and swallows, together with flying insects, including dragonflies: no mean feat. The upper-parts are blue-black with a very distinctive black moustache, white cheeks and white throat. It has a buff-tinged, black-streaked breast and rusty red thighs; the cere and feet are yellow. The call is a shrill 'kek, kek, kek'. No nests have been found in the immediate area, but they do nest in the nearby Usk Valley. There is usually at least one sighting every year of a bird hunting either over local farmland or the young conifer plantations. Old nests of carrion crows in Scots pine are the favoured nesting sites, so one day, maybe? Length 30-36 cm.

The **red-legged partridge** *(Alectoris rufa)* is not a native species, for the British population is descended from released stock. The first recorded attempt at introduction was in the late 17th century, but it wasn't until the late 18th century that any real success was achieved. It can be readily recognised by the conspicuous black, white and chestnut barring on lavender-grey flanks and black spotting below a black band on the upper breast. The lower breast is lavender with buff under-parts; feet and legs are red. The female is slightly duller in colour. The call is a loud 'chuka, chuka'. It is uncommon here, preferring a drier environment than the grey partridge. Any sightings are likely to be releases from shooting groups. Length 34 cm. Resident.

The stoutly built **grey partridge** *(Perdix perdix)* has a tawny chestnut head and throat. The breast and flanks are grey with fine black markings. There are also chestnut bars on the flanks; the upper-parts are brownish buff with vermiculations of black. The male is distinguished from the female by a dark chestnut horseshoe on the lower breast. These birds are gregarious, going about in small coveys. When disturbed they rise abruptly, flying low and fast downwind; their flight consisting of short fast bursts and glides. The usual call is a somewhat grinding but still pleasant 'krrr-ic'. This is another bird that is in serious decline nationally and rarely seen locally. Length 30 cm.

The **common pheasant** *(Phasianus colchicus)* is a native bird of south-west Asia and the Caucasus. The Normans probably introduced it to Britain in the late 11th century. Known as the 'Old English' type, the male has a purple glossed head and neck, lower back and rump mainly rufous; coupled with a long, black-barred reddish buff tail. The females have a general sandy brown appearance and a shorter tail. Later various Far Eastern forms have been introduced with a white-ringed neck and a green rump. These have inter-bred with the 'Old English' type, and other introduced subspecies, so that Britain is now occupied by an amalgam of pheasant forms from all over Asia.

On the wing they are capable of rapid acceleration, climbing steeply to avoid trees or bushes. But they lack the stamina for sustained flight, and when startled often prefer to run. The call of the male is a loud strident 'kor-kok'. It has declined locally over recent years, and any resident population is dependent on pheasant management groups that rear and release birds for shooting. Length 53-89 cm. Resident.

The **moorhen** *(Gallinula chloropus)* is the only waterfowl with a bright red forehead coupled to a red bill

Male lapwing on nest in agricultural set aside

with a yellow tip. The upper-parts are olive brown with a white flash along the flank, the under-parts are grey, and the feet and legs are green. When swimming it scarcely ever stops bobbing its head and flicking its tail, revealing white under-tail coverts. It is a great survivor and practically any patch of water or muddy ditch surrounded by vegetation suits it. These birds are good divers, and when threatened will remain submerged in the water, obtaining air by protruding their bill above the surface. Their flight is weak and rather laboured, with their legs trailing straight out behind. Their main call is a loud frog-like 'kr-rrrk'. Length 33cm. Resident.

The quarrelsome **common coot** *(Fulica atra)* is our only all-black water bird with a conspicuous white forehead and bill and green legs. Largely vegetarian the coot harvests its food from the bottom of the pond, coming to the surface to eat it. It prefers a larger area of water than a moorhen and the only place it appears locally is on the ponds at Loysey, and the Hoop, which is just outside the district. On the wing it exhibits a laboured flight similar to that of a moorhen. The call is a distinctive 'kowk' or 'kewk', the young utter a persistent piping 'kweep'. Length 38cm. Resident.

The **northern lapwing** *(Vanellus vanellus)* is recognised by a long, curved, glossy green-black crest and crown, coupled with an overall black and white appearance. The upper-parts show coppery green in bright sunlight. The tail is white with a sub-terminal black band, the under-tail coverts are a warm chestnut. One of the traditional sights of early spring is the tumbling display flight of a male lapwing. On conspicuously broad rounded wings, it climbs, rolls and falls as if out of control, emitting a rhythmic, wheezy, ecstatic song, accompanied by noisy beatings of the wings. Its calls and song are all variations on a 'peewit' theme; indeed 'peewit' is a vernacular English name. This is another species in serious decline across the country, particularly on farmland. Length 30 cm. Resident.

Coot with newly hatched chick

The **common snipe** *(Gallinago gallinago)* has proportionately the longest bill of any bird here. It is distinguished from the woodcock by its smaller size and black-brown crown divided by a longitudinal buff line. The whole head appears paler than the neck and chest. Plumage is dark brown, flanks are fully barred, the under-parts are pure white and the wings have a prominent white trailing edge, which is obvious in flight. It often appears in small parties, and when disturbed most birds rise suddenly, zigzag close to the ground, and then climb steeply. Sometimes they are seen on a low perch uttering an insistent 'chip-per, chip-per'. They do not nest here, but do feed in the winter in the wet pastures on the edge of Trellech and on Cleddon Bog. Length 27 cm.

The **Eurasian curlew** *(Numenius arquata)* is instantly recognised by its long decurved bill and long legs. The light and dark brown spangled plumage camouflages the bird on open grassland. On the wing, it exhibits a white rump and light brown streaked under-parts. The call 'courlis' or 'kour-lie' has a haunting quality,

Curlew leaving its nest in long grass

nests in holes in trees and it has even been known to nest in rabbit burrows. Length 33 cm. Resident.

The **woodpigeon** *(Columba palumbus)* is distinguished from other pigeons and doves by the conspicuous white patch on the outer wing coverts when in flight, and a white patch on each side of its neck. The head, neck, lower back, rump and tail coverts are bluish grey, with purple and green reflections on the nape and neck. Pigeons are unique among birds in producing a special fluid on which to feed their young; it is generated in the crop, and is analogous to the milk produced by mammals. It is known as crop milk. This ability has an important influence on the birds' ecology. Many birds are dependent on good supplies of seasonal food when feeding their young. The ability to produce this milk removes any such seasonal dependence, and so they can breed over a longer period. Flight is fast and direct. When displaying they rise in an arc, perform wing claps and then glide down on bowed wings. Their song, giving a promise of eternal devotion, is a soothing 'coo-coo-coo-coo-coo'. Length 40-42 cm. Resident.

The **collared dove** *(Streptopelia decaocta)* is a relative newcomer to Britain, first nesting here in 1955. It is now widespread throughout the country. This rapid colonisation has been one of the most dramatic events witnessed by present-day ornithologists. Until about 1930 these doves were restricted in Europe to Turkey and parts of the Balkans. They are great opportunists, regularly visiting gardens for food. They are a pale greyish buff with subtle areas of pale pink and blue-grey. The adult birds have a half ring of black at the back of the neck. The underside of the tail has a black base and large white tip. Usual song is a lively repeated 'cuk-coo-cuk'. Length 32 cm. Resident.

The magnificent **barn owl** *(Tyto alba)* is easily distinguished from other owls by its buff and white colour. The orange-golden buff of the upper-parts is delicately patterned with grey, white and brown. The heart-shaped face is white, and the breast is either pure

vividly evocative of the wilder moorland places and the coastal mudflats it inhabits elsewhere in Britain. The trilling, tremulous song, delivered on the wing in the breeding season, is full of wild beauty and is the favourite song of many birdwatchers. Rising and falling in a delicate, fluttering flight it produces a series of liquid bubbling notes, as it hangs, then glides slowly earthward to land. This is a bird that has declined markedly over the last decade as a local breeding species. This decline is undoubtedly exacerbated by the shift in emphasis from hay to silage production, the spring silage cut occurring at the height of the breeding season, which results in the destruction of many nests. Length 53-58 cm. Resident.

The **stock dove** *(Columba oenas)* is smaller and shorter tailed than a woodpigeon and a bluer grey in colour with no white patches. These birds have two short black wing bars and black wing tips; the feet are a bright pinkish red. They are uncommon but their far carrying song - a grunting double 'coo'- and their display flight makes location easy. It is the only European pigeon that

Tranquility, a pair of collared doves

white or lightly tinged with buff. It has a very upright stance, standing on rather spindly legs that have a rather 'knock-kneed' appearance. When flying at dusk the barn owl is seen as a ghostly elusive form, its slow hunting flight being buoyant and wavering. A barn owl can sometimes be seen during the day, especially when feeding its young.

The call is a prolonged, strangled, almost blood curdling screech. The Revd Gilbert White is quoted as saying:

> *I have known a whole village up in arms on such an occasion, imagining the churchyard to be full of goblins and spectres.*

They also hiss and snore. When alarmed they make a snapping noise with their mandibles. This is yet again another species that has declined locally and nationally, but they do breed occasionally here. Length 34 cm. Resident.

The **little owl** (*Athene noctua*) is not an indigenous British species. It was introduced during the late 19th century. It is distinguished from the other owls by its small size and whitish spots on a greyish brown head and wings; underparts are a dull white with brown streaks. It has a short tail and a conspicuously bounding flight. As one of the more diurnal owls, it will often be seen sitting on a post or other prominent perch during the day. The call is a loud ringing 'kiew, kiew, kiew'. Habitually uttered during the day, the song is remarkably like the opening sequence of the curlew. This is another species that has recently been much less in evidence locally. Length 22 cm.

The **common swift** (*Apus apus*) is easily distinguished from the swallow by its short tail and long, narrow, scythe-like wings. They are brownish-black in colour with a dull white throat. This throat colouring is rather more obvious in juveniles, which also have pale tips to their wings. The swift is the most aerial of all birds, feeding,

Young barn owl waiting to be fed

mating and even sleeping on the wing. Their diet is composed entirely of aerial insects caught with a fully open gape.

Observations have shown that they regularly feed at heights of over 1000 metres. Their eyes are set deep in the feathers, and they get extra protection from airborne debris by a set of bristles. They have four small needle-sharp claws on each foot, all pointing forward, to enable them to cling on to vertical surfaces. Locally they nest under the eaves or in some small fissure in the church and older buildings in Trellech. They can be seen feeding over the local countryside but they are known to travel prodigious distances from the nest. Their nest material, which includes straw and feathers, is gathered on the wing and cemented together with saliva. Swifts have a vigorous dashing flight best seen when excited; squealing parties chase each other round the buildings. Normal utterance is a familiar harsh scream. Length 16.5 cm. Summer visitor.

The **skylark** (*Alauda arvensis*) is very much a bird of the open fields. It feeds entirely on the ground. The upper-parts are buffish brown, streaked with darker brown, while the under-parts are pale buff with brown streaks. It has an often inconspicuous crest, except when alarmed. On the wing it can be recognised by an ample triangular-shaped wing with pale trailing edges. Its song though is its best field mark, notable not only for the quality of the trills, warbles and mimetic passages, but also for its duration. It can last for several minutes. This ethereal song, delivered non-stop while climbing an invisible spiral stairway to such a height that the bird is barely visible to the naked eye, has inspired our greatest poets throughout the ages, the best known being:

Hail to thee blithe Spirit!
Bird thou never wert,
That from Heaven or near it,
Pourest thy full heart
In profuse strains of unpremeditated art.

Ode to a Skylark by PERCY BYSHE SHELLEY

Its numbers have seriously declined over recent years, both locally and nationally. Length 18 cm. Resident.

The **barn swallow** (*Hirundo rustica*) has been a welcome guest of human habitation from the earliest times, and is probably the most familiar of our summer visitors. Their arrival in early April heralds the spring. They are slim, narrow-winged birds with the outer feathers of the forked tail on the adult tapering into streamers; the juveniles have a shorter fork. The head and upper-parts are a glossy steel blue, coupled with a reddish chestnut forehead and throat. There is a blue-black band across the lower throat, and the under-parts are a buff or creamy white. Few birds are so at home on the wing as the swallow. They fly low, feeding over open ground, particularly pastures with horses and cattle, with a lithesome, flowing action that no other bird matches.

And here's the swallow, wild and free,
Prince flyer of the air by day.

Newcomers by W.H. DAVIES

The song is a musical twittering 'tswit, tswit, tswit'. When alarmed near its nest site the bird utters a shrill double "tsink, tsink", as it swoops towards the intruder. Length 19 cm.

Male swallow feeding offspring in an adopted nest

The Potential Problems of Nesting Barn Swallows

Last year, true to form, a pair of swallows returned to nest in their ancestral home in our barn, which for at least 10 years has housed a single nest. The same nest has been carefully refurbished each year. Despite the generally poor spring and summer weather, successive generations have always managed to raise two broods successfully. The barn is of steel construction, open on one side. The nest is rather difficult to see, sited high up in the apex of the roof, between two longitudinal beams. Considered by many to be the real herald of spring, the swallows arrived on 24 April and immediately advertised their presence, with the male delivering an extended rendition of his delightful, friendly, twittering song from the television aerial on the house, their favourite perch. I call this their favourite perch because this has been where successive pairs have regularly consummated their relationships.

The serious nest building and refurbishment did not start in earnest until the second week in May, but in the meantime they kept us enthralled with their aerial skills as they flew around the house and barn. Then their efforts to refurbish the nest were stepped up, with mud collected from the well-paddled, muddy areas that surrounded the animal drinking troughs in the adjacent fields, and from a small puddle on our drive. This construction work was conducted in regular bursts of activity throughout the day. By the end of the week, I knew the work was nearing completion when I saw them flying in with feathers to line the nest. On one occasion the male dropped a feather he was carrying, and the female immediately dived to recover it, then dropped it again only for the male to recover it. This highly skilled and apparently playful routine went on for fully two to three minutes before they finally retrieved the feather and carried it to the nest. I construed this to be an instinctive celebration of a job well done and considered myself privileged to have had a ringside seat. All went relatively quiet then for two to three weeks as the egg laying and incubation took place. I first became aware they were feeding young when I found an eggshell on the ground close to the nest. It was cut perfectly in half across its length, characterising a successfully hatched egg.

After about 10 days of non-stop feeding, we had a spell of extremely hot weather and I observed that the young birds were hanging over the edge of the nest with their beaks wide open trying to cool themselves. The fact that the nest was in the apex of the roof of the steel barn could only have exacerbated the heat problem, with the result that the air temperature must have been in excess of 100 degrees Fahrenheit over the midday period. On going into the barn after two further days of extreme heat I found two fledglings on the ground under the nest. I suspected the excess heat had triggered the fall. They probably fell while jostling each other in attempting to take advantage of the increase in airflow at the edge of the nest. Fearing that they would become victims to our recently acquired stray cat if left on the barn floor - and concerned that if I climbed up to the nest to return them I might induce the other three fledglings to fall out - I placed them on a cross beam on the side wall of the barn about three metres above the ground. I stood back to see if the parent birds would find them.

My concerns soon evaporated, for the next time the hen bird flew in to the barn the two fledglings became very vociferous and animated. After a couple of fly-pasts the mother alighted and fed them. But soon after she had left, they became restless and started to shuffle along the beam on their weak legs, and inevitably toppled onto the floor again. What next, I wondered? Then I remembered I had an unoccupied open-fronted nest-box on the end of the barn, so I removed it and nailed it to the beam identified earlier, perched the two fledglings on the front edge, and awaited the outcome. When the adults returned they flew straight to the nest in the apex of the roof, leaving me thinking they were not going to feed the two 'itinerants' in the nest-box. However, when the male returned for

A male swallow carrying food for its young

the second time, he appeared to make an attempt to feed them in the nest box but then veered away and fed the youngsters in the natural nest. This routine was repeated several times by both adults during successive feeding visits, during which time the 'itinerants' were becoming extremely agitated about their lack of food. It then occurred to me that the overhang on the nest-box roof could be the problem, as there was insufficient headroom for the adults to alight and feed them.

I removed the nest-box roof and the next time the adults entered the barn they went straight to the nest-box and fed them. All five youngsters were successfully reared in their respective abodes, although I should add the 'itinerants' were the first to fly.

I am pleased to report they returned the following April, and within minutes of arrival they were twittering away in the barn close to the old nest, obviously discussing a refurbishment programme. I will watch with interest.

The gregarious **house martin** *(Delichon urbica)* has a prominent white rump, which is its best field mark. The upper-parts are a glossy dark blue and the under-parts a brilliant white. The forked tail is shorter than that of a swallow. On the wing they have a flicking action. Like the swallow the house martin has a close association with man, the great majority of its nests being built under the eaves of houses, and was well known to William Shakespeare:

> *This guest of summer,*
> *The temple-haunting martlet, does approve,*
> *By his loved mansionry, that the heaven's breath*
> *Smells wooingly here: no jutty, frieze,*
> *Buttress, nor coigne of vantage, but this bird*
> *Hath made his pendent bed and procreant cradle:*
> *Where they most breed and haunt, I have observed*
> *The air is delicate.*

From *Macbeth* by WILLIAM SHAKESPEARE

Where possible they nest in colonies; the largest local one is at Hygga, where up to 50 pairs nest under the eaves on a farmhouse. The usual call is something like 'chirr-up'. Variations of this compose the song, uttered by the bird in its nest, perched outside it, and on the wing. Length 12.5 cm. Summer visitor.

The slender **yellow wagtail** *(Motacilla flava)* is smaller and has a shorter tail than our other wagtails. The male can be distinguished from the grey wagtail by a greenish yellow crown, mantle, and a yellow eye-stripe. The under-parts are bright yellow; wings and tail are blackish brown with white outer tail feathers, grey lesser wing coverts and rather inconspicuous white wing-bars. The females are duller and the yellow under-parts are very pale. It is a graceful and dainty walker, but rather tense and nervous in manner. The call note is a compelling shrill 'tsweep, tsweep'. This repeated note, once memorised, identifies the presence of the bird long before it is seen, the carrying power being very intrusive; few bird calls have the same capacity for demanding attention. It is very much a bird of moist lowland pastures below 150 metres and hence it has rarely been seen locally. Two pairs did breed successfully here in 1997, at an altitude of 215 metres. This was the first proven breeding for at least 20 years. One or two pairs have bred regularly here since, favouring fields of grass and potatoes for nest sites. Length 16.5 cm. Summer visitor.

The **grey wagtail** *(Motacilla cinerea)* is the most graceful of our wagtails. Its nimble actions and handsome plumage lend enjoyment to a walk by a flowing stream. It frequents the Penarth brook, which starts in Trellech and flows through the Woolpitch and Liyna woods to the south-west. It can be recognised by its uniform slate-blue upper-parts, very long tail, yellow-green rump, sulphur yellow under-parts and white outer tail feathers. Juveniles have a slightly speckled breast and are only really yellow on the under tail coverts. Unlike other wagtails they often perch in trees, making sorties to catch passing insects. The call note is a staccato, metallic 'tsiz-it'. Length 18 cm. Resident.

A male yellow wagtail carrying food for its young

Grey wagtail with a melange of mayflies for its nestlings

A winter visiting redwing sated on holly berries

The **pied wagtail** *(Motacilla alba)* is easily recognised by its black, white and grey plumage, black rump and long black tail with white outer feathers. They are regularly seen walking on roofs or walls with a deliberate, stepping gait, head bobbing and tail wagging, coupled with swift dashes after insects. The flight note is a distinctive high-pitched 'tschizzick'. They have a twittering song, which may be delivered on the wing, or on the ground. Outside of the breeding season they roost communally in bushes or buildings, sometimes in assemblies of several hundred. Length 18 cm. Resident.

The **fieldfare** *(Turdus pilaris)* is easily separated from the other thrushes of the area by the combination of a blue-grey head and rump and chestnut brown back, but in flight at a distance it resembles a mistle thrush, having the same white under-wing flashes. They like to perch on top of the highest trees, always very alert and rather wary. Like the redwing they can be seen feeding in flocks in the fields, usually well spread out either on their own or in the company of other thrushes. The call note is a distinctive harsh chuckling 'tchak'. Length 25 cm. Winter visitor.

The smallest of our thrushes, the **redwing** *(Turdus iliacus)* is easily recognised by a white stripe over the eye, brown upper-parts and conspicuous reddish chestnut flanks and under-wing. On approach, the birds utter a pretty lisping 'twip', whereas the flight note is a very high-pitched 'seeih'. In the winter months, they can be seen feeding in the fields in flocks of 40-50, and sometimes in larger mixed flocks with fieldfares and mistle thrushes. Length 21 cm. Winter visitor and passage migrant.

The handsome **northern wheatear** *(Oenanthe oenanthe)* derives its name from the Anglo-Saxon words meaning 'white rump', which is a very conspicuous feature when the bird flies. The male has mostly grey upper-parts, buff breast

Right: Close up of a male pied wagtail, showing the beauty of black and white

and white under-parts, black ear coverts with a white stripe passing round the forehead and over the eyes; the wings and end of the tail are black. The female has brown upper-parts and ear coverts coupled with buff-white under-parts. They haunt open areas, and have a habit of perching on small eminences, making themselves conspicuous. The usual call note is a stony 'chack' or 'weet-chack, chack', the song is a thin warble. They are passage birds seen in the spring most years. I always considered the habitat around Hygga was suitable for nesting, and 'eureka', in the summer of 2000 a pair nested on the ridge there, but unfortunately they were not successful. I suspect that weasels robbed the nest. Length 15 cm.

The **dipper** (*Cinclus cinclus*) sometimes known as the water ousel, is a lover of tree-covered, fast-running streams. It is a sturdy dark brown, white-throated bird, readily described as a large wren. Like the wren, it has a conspicuously short tail. It is further characterised by its continuous bobbing action on the water's edge or on rocks in the middle of the water. It walks underwater on the stream bed, feeding mainly on larval forms of water beetles, alder flies and dragonflies, as well as water snails and occasionally small fish. Owing to this diet, its presence on waterways has been identified as a good indicator of the purity of the water. It builds a large domed nest similar to a wren. These are often built on man-made structures under bridges, in culverts or on walls, while others are marvellously camouflaged amongst tree roots or overhanging vegetation. Like the grey wagtail it can also be seen on the Penarth brook. The song is a cheerful, meditative warble. Length 18 cm. Resident.

The **magpie** (*Pica pica*) is easily recognised by its black and white plumage with green and purple reflections and a long graduated tail. Flight is weaker than other crows, appearing slightly unbalanced by its long tail. On the ground it walks energetically or hops. Magpies are notorious as predators of eggs and young birds. The most common call of the magpie is a harsh machine gun like rattle. It has been described as 'a hoarse rapid shushushushu'. Length 46 cm. Resident.

Bird Brain

One autumn day I started putting a small ball of fat out for the birds to supplement their diet of peanuts. I hung it from a branch of a tree on a piece of string about 30 cm long. It very quickly attracted the attention of a couple of young magpies, but finding a way of accessing the fat posed problems for them. They first tried pecking at the string at the point where it was tied to the branch, but this proved unsuccessful. They then tried to reach the fat by stretching down from the branch, and then they tried pecking at it as they dropped past it from the branch to the ground. Once again they had no luck, and their attempts become more and more frenetic. Eventually they flew off frustrated.

I thought they would come back and sure enough they did, going through the same routines a number of times each day over a period of about a week. During this time they tried a further variation, flying up to the fatball from the ground, and trying to peck it. This also proved ineffective, although they did manage to pick off some small crumbs. Then one day I noticed the young birds had brought in the 'heavy gang' in the shape of a mature magpie. Its approach was more relaxed, and after a couple of abortive attempts at trying to reach the fat by leaning down from the branch, it took hold of the supporting string in its beak a couple of centimetres below the branch and pulled it up, raising the fatball. It then tried to repeat this action, but on opening its beak it dropped it again. It did this a few times, and then 'eureka' it leaned down, took hold of the string, drew it up and put its foot on the loose loop. It then repeated this action a number of times until it had the fatball in its beak.

Full of admiration for the performance, I pondered how I could deter the magpie, and still leave the fat accessible for the small birds. I came to the conclusion that lengthening the string might solve the problem, so I suspended the fatball on a piece of string 90 cm long.

Right: Dipper in typical watery surroundings showing the 'scaly' markings on the feathers

This quickly proved to be no deterrent. On its next visit the mature bird had a couple of abortive attempts to reach the fat, but it was soon pulling up the string and feeding. Young birds were still visiting, and watching as the mature magpie went through its successful routine, but they did not appear to learn from its actions, they still kept going through their old failed routines.

I then decided to withdraw the fat for a couple of weeks, and then to reintroduce it when the magpies stopped visiting. The unanswered question is, was this magpie exhibiting 'learned behaviour' or was it an example of 'trial and error' built on past experience, or was it showing the ability to reason?

The **Eurasian jackdaw** *(Corvus monedula)* is well entrenched in European folklore and literature, and in keeping with some other crows it has a liking for bright objects, as related in this poem.

That, heedless of grammar, they all cried, "That's him!
That's the scamp that has done this scandalous thing!
That's the thief that has got my Lord Cardinal's ring!
The poor little Jackdaw, when the monks he saw
Feebly gave vent to the ghost of a Caw
And turned his bald head, as much as to say
Pray, be so good as to walk this way!
Slower and slower he limped on before
Till they came to the back of the belfry door
Where the first they saw, midst the sticks with the straw
Was the ring in the nest of that little Jackdaw!

From *The Jackdaw of Rheims* – anonymous

It is the smallest black crow; its defining characteristic is a glossy metallic blue head and a grey nape. Jackdaws are very aerobatic flyers with a faster wing beat than larger crows. The characteristic calls are 'ky-ah' or 'ka' or 'chack'. They have a troublesome habit of nesting in chimneys. Length 33 cm. Resident.

The intensely gregarious **rook** *(Corvus frugilegus)* nests in rookeries and is regularly seen with jackdaws. It is all black, with a violet gloss, and the adults have conspicuous pale skin at the base of the bill. The upper part of the leg is heavily feathered, giving it a 'baggy trousers' look a characteristic that separates it from the carrion crow. Its flight is rather laboured, and on the ground it walks rather sedately. The harsh 'caw' or 'caah' calls are more deliberate and prolonged than those of the carrion crow. There are no rookeries in the region, but the birds can be seen foraging in local fields. Length 46 cm. Resident.

The **carrion crow** *(Corvus corone)* is increasingly common throughout the area. It is all black with purple and green reflections, and the tail is square ended. Unlike the rook, its thigh feathers are tight fitting. Crows are usually seen singly or in pairs, but will flock, especially to roost.

Light thickens; and the crow makes wing to the
rooky wood.

From *Macbeth* by WILLIAM SHAKESPEARE

The main call is a hoarse 'kaaah', which is often repeated three times. It has a slow flapping flight, and on the ground, it walks and sidles with ungainly hops. Length 47 cm. Resident.

The heavy-billed **common raven** *(Corvus corax)* has bristling throat feathers and is the largest all-black bird of the region. The tail is wedge shaped, and the adult bird is similar in size to a buzzard. It flies rather heavily on fingered wings, but in the spring can be seen performing remarkable aerobatics on the up-currents over Beacon Hill, tumbling, rolling, flying upside down and nose-diving. On the ground it walks rather majestically. The main call is a deep croaking 'pruk, pruk, pruk'. Length 64 cm. Resident.

The croaking raven doth bellow for revenge.

From *Hamlet* by WILLIAM SHAKESPEARE

Ravens, the dominant group member takes its fill

When viewed in bright sunlight the plumage of the **common starling** *(Sturnus vulgaris)* male is glossy black with metallic reflections of purples, greens and blues, whereas the female is duller. The bill is a bright yellow in the spring, but it turns dark in the late summer; its base is bluish in the male and pinkish in the female. When flying it appears fat-bodied with a distinct arrowhead shape. It has a very quick wing action. Highly gregarious, starlings roost communally in very large numbers in trees, reed beds and on buildings in city centres. The starling's familiar song is a curious medley of whistles, clicks, 'twips', 'guks' and other chattering sounds. When uttered in concert by large numbers in a roost these notes compose a symphony. The usual cry is a harsh 'kwrrr' when the bird is disturbed. This is another species that is in decline locally and nationally. Length 21.5 cm. Resident.

The **house sparrow** *(Passer domesticus)* is the archetypal brown bird renowned for its cheeky opportunism. An ash-grey crown and rump, a black chin and throat, chestnut mantle and lores distinguish the male. The female is undistinguished except for a single pale wing-bar. It is highly gregarious, inhabiting human settlements of all kinds. The sparrow has a considerable vocabulary, but the most familiar call is 'chilp'. Sparrows are in serious decline. They have suffered on farmland following the introduction of mechanisation that has reduced the corn available in stubble and in the farmyard after harvesting. Length 14.5 cm. Resident.

The neat **tree sparrow** *(Passer montanus)* is similar to a house sparrow, but smaller with a chocolate brown crown and nape, a black patch on a white cheek, a small black throat bib and a double white wing-bar. The sexes are alike. It is most likely to be seen on areas of farmland that have hedgerows with old mature trees with nesting holes, or on the woodland edge. The call note is a quick high pitched 'chip, chip, chip' and the

Wary tree sparrow visiting nest site in elder trunk

characteristic flight note is 'teck, teck, teck'; the flight is very direct. It is now scarce and any recent sightings have been in the south of the region around Hygga. This decline reflects what is happening nationally. Length 14 cm. Resident.

The **goldfinch** *(Carduelis carduelis)* is probably the prettiest of our native birds and is instantly recognised by the crimson face, white and black head, whitish rump and a bright golden yellow wing-bar. The juvenile birds are brown streaked and lack any red, white or black on the face. A goldfinch has a long, thin, pointed bill, which it inserts into the heads of such plants as thistles, teasel and knapweed to extract the seeds. The characteristic, twittering flight calls aid identification. The song is a series of cheerful, tinkling variations of 'tswitt-witt-witt'. It was because of this cheerful song and its attractive plumage that it suffered considerable persecution in Britain in the 19th and early 20th century, when thousands were caught and sold as cage birds. This practice still goes on in parts of Europe. Length 12 cm.

In addition to the birds reviewed tufted duck, little grebe, kingfisher, and peregrine falcon, have all been seen occasionally. There are also irregular visits of flocks of seabirds, made up of common gull, lesser black-backed gull and herring gull, and a great cormorant has been seen flying over Beacon Hill on its way to the River Wye at Monmouth.

Over the last 25 years there have also been recorded sightings of a number of scarce visitors to the county, namely honey buzzard, red kite, hoopoe, firecrest, and great grey shrike. In the spring of 1996 I saw a black-eared wheatear in Ninewells Wood, but unfortunately this sighting, a county first, was not officially ratified. A juvenile male ring ouzel was seen on Beacon Hill in late September 1999; this was probably on passage from Scandinavia to its winter quarters in Spain or North Africa. This was my first sighting of this species here since moving here in 1975. It stayed feeding in our garden on Beacon Hill for about a week before moving on.

This ramble through the bird life of the area will hopefully convey to all readers the variety of birds that can be seen in a small district of Monmouthsire. I would also like to think it will remind them how lucky they are to visit or reside in one of Britain's most beautiful settings.

These sightings highlight the excitement of birdwatching, and what can be seen by the observant and inquiring observer. Every time you go out, there is always the possibility you may see a rarity or maybe even a county first, or just a common bird behaving in an unusual manner.

And many a charming truth will I discover,
How birds after a wetting in the rain,
Can make their notes come twice as sweet; and then
How sparrows hop with both their legs together
While pigeons stride leg after leg, like men.

From the poem *The Song of Life* by W.H. DAVIES

Glimpse of the Sun

On one soggy summer's day, in one of the wettest Augusts' on record, a local resident from Catbrook village rang and asked me if I would like to photograph a bird that had recently appeared in her garden. A local expert had identified it as a male **mariqua sunbird** *(Nectarino mariquensis).*

It was an offer I couldn't refuse. Although it wasn't ringed, I assumed it had escaped from a private aviary. The brightly coloured, highly active members of the sunbird *(Nectariniidae)* group are a very distinctive family of small nectar-loving birds with long tongues for imbibing nectar, coupled with a long decurved beak for probing into flowers. They are also insectivorous. The males have patches of iridescent feathers which range in colour from scarlet to blue, orange, yellow, green, bronze and violet. They are the Old World equivalent of the New World humming-birds, but unlike humming-birds, they do not hover to feed, but alight on the plants to extract the nectar.

In this alien environment our escapee had identified the flowers of montbretia as a source of food. Fittingly this is a plant that was introduced into this country from

Goldfinches feeding on thistle seeds

the Old World; and it was feeding on montbretia when I arrived to take its photograph. What I found fascinating was that owing to the patches of iridescent feathers, any attempt to provide a simple description of the bird's colour was extremely difficult. Any observed colour was transitory and totally dependent on the angle of light at that instant. This colour conundrum was further compounded by the bird's hyperactivity. The conundrum was solved by the action-stopping, fast shutter speed of the camera. The resulting photograph revealed that the bird had a petrol blue mantle and a patterned, brightly coloured gorget.

It stayed around the garden for about a week before disappearing, its fate unknown. Unfortunately, one certainty is that it would not have survived for long in the wild in this country, particularly at a time of the year with dropping temperatures and dwindling nectar sources.

An escaped mariqua sunbird on montbretia

Part Two — *Other Vertebrates*

Compared with birdwatching, sighting other vertebrates is more difficult. It demands greater effort and patience, coupled with a good knowledge of their habits. The majority of wild animals are shy, have a keen sense of smell and will usually detect you and move away before you see them. Normally they stay under cover in daylight, only venturing out into the open after dark. Consequently, few are likely to be seen during the day.

For this reason it is imperative that anybody who wants to see them acquires some knowledge of their habitats and breeding cycles, as well as some basic skills in identifying a few of the telltale signs they leave behind.

To the observant eye, there are numerous signs that reveal the presence of a number of the larger species. Namely the type of track left in the mud or snow, droppings, wisps of hair caught on fencing wire. The height of the snag will provide clues as to what animal was there. The presence of some of the smaller animals can be established and identified by teeth mark patterns left on opened hazelnut shells, or on gnawed pine-cones and rose-hips.

The following animals of the area are based on my own observations. I have not attempted to place them into clearly defined habitats, but simply stated where they may be found or seen. Many sightings were opportunistic - and in some cases isolated - so no definite conclusions should be drawn on how common or widespread the particular animals are, unless stated otherwise.

Chapter 7
The *mammals*

The **red fox** *(Vulpes vulpes)* is common throughout the district, and looks like a slim prick-eared dog. It is the only wild relative of the dog in Britain. Its coat colouring varies from yellow-brown to red-brown, the lower legs and ears are black and its bushy tail often has a white tip. It also has very distinctive amber eyes. Alert, wary, cunning and stealthy as a cat, it has very acute hearing coupled with a keen sense of smell.

Or to see the subtle fox,
How the villain plies the box:
After feeding on his prey,
How he closely sneaks away,
Through the hedge and down the furrow
Till he gets into his burrow:

From the poem *The Happy Countryman*
by N. BRETON

Foxes are mostly active at night, when they forage for food, killing small mammals particularly rabbits and voles, while also scavenging from dustbins and carcasses of animals killed on the roads.

To the detriment of farmers, they will also kill lambs and poultry, although certain vociferous national groups of people would have us believe differently. Always the opportunist they will also eat berries, beetles, eggs and young birds when available.

A den or 'earth' is used at breeding time, and this usually has several entrance holes. The fox may dig the burrows but often a deserted badger's sett is used. A large burrow complex is sometimes occupied by both species at the same time. Fox cubs, in litters of three to five, are born in mid-March, emerging from the den for the first time at five or six weeks old. They quickly learn to hunt, and after a further four to five weeks are ready to leave the earth. The usual call is a bark like a dog, but with a higher and sharper note. The vixen utters an eerie scream during the mating season in January or February. A couple of years ago I took a walk at dusk to Whitestones by way of Bluegates when a vixen's scream came from the undergrowth just a few metres from me. For a few seconds I believed in ghosts - and the hairs on the back of my neck not only stood up, but ran for cover. A fully grown red fox is 58-85 cm long, stands 35-55 cm high at the shoulder, tail length 35-55 cm and weighs 3-8 kg.

The **badger** *(Meles meles)*, common here, is primarily nocturnal, although it will emerge for short periods in the day in secluded places.

In the late 1980s, I was walking the dog on Beacon Hill in full daylight at about 7 o'clock one morning, when I heard a disturbance in the undergrowth. The dog started barking excitedly. I took a closer look and in a small one metre clearing amidst the vegetation, which was in shadow, there was a fully grown badger. Its body was fully visible, but I could not see its head which was pointed away from me and pushed deep into a very dense patch of vegetation, so I presume it could not see me. I leaned over and touched it a couple of times, and on each occasion it made a growling noise and pushed its head

Foraging badgers

deeper into the vegetation. So rather than cause it any further discomfort, I walked away. I took the dog home and returned about half an hour later, but it had gone. I can only think it had sought sanctuary in the undergrowth when it heard the dog, and sticking its head into a dark patch of vegetation lulled it into a false sense of security.

Badgers have a barrel-shaped body, short powerful legs with strong claws, and a short blunt tail. Its coat consists of rather stiff, coarse hairs, which are whitish with a black band just short of the tip giving it a silver-grey appearance. Its legs and under-parts are black, but its most distinctive feature is its white head that has a black stripe over each ear and eye.

> *The badger grunting on his woodland track*
> *With shaggy hide and sharp nose scrowed with black*
> *Roots in the bushes and the woods and makes*
> *A great hugh burrow in the ferns and brake*
> *With nose on ground he runs a awkward pace*
> *And anything will beat him in the race*

From the poem *The Badger* by JOHN CLARE

A badger's diet is very varied. In fact it is often described as omnivorous. Earthworms form a large part of the diet in the spring; in the summer, many kinds of insects, snails, frogs, eggs and juvenile ground-nesting birds, hedgehogs and other small mammals are eaten. In the early 1990s badgers robbed the eggs from a curlew's nest sited in the grass fields directly below Trellech Beacon. This was the last time curlews attempted to nest there. Nests of bees and wasps are also dug out, and the grubs eaten, as are large amounts of plant food. Life centres on its underground home or sett. This is made up of numerous chambers and tunnels with several entrances. There is a large sett on the roadside on Greenway Hill. Up to five young are usually born in early spring, and stay with their parents until autumn. Length 60-90 cm, tail 11-20 cm, weight usually10-15 kg.

The **stoat** *(Mustela erminea)* is one of our most aggressive predators. Active day and night, they pursue their prey relentlessly in a bounding gait using their excellent hearing and sense of smell. Alert and inquisitive, a stoat often sits up to view its surroundings, revealing the clear division between its creamy-white underside and brown flanks. The tail has a distinctive black tip. Their diet is mainly rabbit, augmented by smaller mammals such as mice, rats, voles, shrews and the eggs and young of ground- nesting birds. Their den is usually in a stone wall, rock crevice or old rabbit burrow. Between three and seven young are born in April or May, and become independent in about 10 weeks. Stoats are preyed on by owls and raptors. Length 38-40 cm, weight 150-200 gm.

The **weasel** *(Mustela nivalis)* is Britain's smallest carnivore and is a fierce hunter. Mice are one of its main foods so farmers and foresters should view it as a friend. Because of its small size, it can follow mice and voles down their burrows. Rabbits, rats and small birds are also eaten if the opportunity arises; prey is dispatched by a bite to the back of the neck.

I once had the privileged and unusual experience of standing quietly in a hedgerow bird-watching when two young weasels exploded excitedly out of a nearby hole under some exposed tree roots. They proceeded to chase each other in and out of the roots for several minutes, running over my feet several times in the process, before disappearing back down the hole. They were obviously completely oblivious of my presence. Its long slim body has chestnut-coloured fur above, and white under-parts. Between four and seven young are born in a nest of grass in a hole, tree stump or crevice; there are usually two litters a year. Length 25 cm, tail 5 cm, weight 50-80 gm.

One hundred years ago the **polecat** *(Mustela putorius),* once called the 'foul-mart' because of its strong smell, was found all over Britain, but, as a result of persecution, it is now confined to Wales and the borders. It was trapped both for its fur (fitch) and because it was considered a threat to game and poultry. There have been isolated sightings locally over recent years, suggesting it is making a comeback, but the picture is clouded by the number of escaped polecat-ferrets living wild. The ferret is a domesticated form of polecat, whose exact origin is uncertain but is possibly derived from the East European form. Polecats are mainly nocturnal and prey on rabbits, small mammals, reptiles, frogs, young birds and eggs, located mainly by scent and hearing. They usually live in

The ubiquitous grey squirrel taking advantage of the autumn fruits

home we have had personal experience of this, as we had two 20-year-old trees in the garden ringed in 2002 - an oak and a sycamore. Both died. They also eat insects and the eggs and young of birds.

Commonly called the 'tree rat' they have survived several government-sanctioned attempts at extermination by shooting, trapping and poison. They are extremely resourceful and intelligent, surviving in hedgerow trees, gardens and other places without large areas of trees. A squirrel's winter coat appears mainly grey with light under-parts and a yellowish brown streak along the back. In the summer it looks more brownish with yellowish brown feet and flanks. Its bushy grizzled tail stays the same colour all year. Hairy ear tufts visible in the winter disappear in the summer. If the weather and feeding conditions are favourable squirrels will usually produce two litters of three or four young in the spring or early summer in a treetop drey or nest made of leafy twigs and lined with grass. Their presence is often revealed by a loud 'churring' noise as they aggressively scold or chase off an intruder. Length 24-30 cm, tail 10-25 cm, weight 510-570 gm.

woods or hedgerows in old rabbit burrows, or among tree roots, where the female - called a Jill - gives birth to four to six young in March or April, there are possibly two litters a year. It has creamy yellow under-fur protected by long dark guard hairs, and may vary in colour from pale to almost black. Length 45-65 cm, including a tail of 13-19 cm. Weight: Males up to 1500 gm, female up to 800 gm.

The most common and most often seen mammal here is the **grey squirrel** *(Sciurus carolinensis)*, a native of the hardwood forests of the United States. It was misguidedly introduced into Britain in the mid 19th century, and is now widespread throughout. Although seen by many members of the public as an attractive and endearing creature, grey squirrels do considerable damage in commercial woodlands, where they eat the leaves, young shoots, buds and flowers, and also attack the main branches and trunks of trees, tearing off the bark to access the sappy layers underneath.

Sometimes the tree is completely ringed and dies. At

Salad Days

While out walking on a beautiful spring-like day in early February, I noticed a grey squirrel scratching and digging on a grassy bank on the woodland edge. Stopping to watch, I noticed it appeared to take something from where it was digging and started to eat. After a few seconds it did the same again, so I suspected it had a cache of nuts.

But when I focused on it with my binoculars, I could see it was eating a green leaf. It sat in a typical position for a feeding squirrel, holding the leaf between its two front paws and chewing furiously. Having finished the leaf, it repeated the exercise twice more. At this juncture something disturbed it, and it dropped the leaf it was eating and headed for the nearest tree.

Curious to know exactly what it had been eating I wandered over to find the squirrel had been eating the leaves of a **cat's-ear plant** *(Hypochoeris radicata).* Looking at what was left of the plant it must have eaten at least three whole leaves and the parts of several others. This is an erect perennial plant, growing up to 60 cm tall, with a basal rosette of lance-shaped, blunt-toothed, hairy leaves, and a yellow dandelion-like flower. It is a common grassland plant favouring mildly acid soils, and can be used as a salad plant in winter.

I was aware that, in addition to nuts, squirrels eat beech mast, tree shoots, roots, insects, eggs and young nestlings, but I had never seen or heard of them eating leaves like these. I wonder if squirrels are expanding their diets, or was this just a case of normal behaviour, possibly not recorded before? Or, maybe the government's advice that we should eat five portions of vegetables a day is currently under investigation in the animal kingdom!

Cat's-ear plant remains

It was probably the Romans who introduced the **fallow deer** *(Dama dama)* into Britain from Asia Minor, although some authorities consider the species may also have been native to the Mediterranean area of Europe.

Its numbers have increased locally in recent years, probably due to increased movement from the Forest of Dean, and it is now fairly common in the woods in the east of the area. Although it may be seen grazing in the fields at the woodland edges during the day it is generally rather shy and retiring. The deer's main feeding activity starts in the evening and ends soon after dawn. By day they rest and ruminate in the younger forest plantations.

During the summer the buck and doe keep apart, but in the rutting season from the middle of October and throughout the winter they herd together. The doe gives birth to a single fawn in June.

Like all deer, the stags shed their antlers in early spring or summer, and have new ones fully grown in late summer or early autumn before rutting begins. Their diet consists mainly of grasses, herbaceous plants, seeds and berries as well as the foliage of trees and bushes. They do considerable damage in young forest plantations, and private gardens on the woodland edge. The ground colour of the summer coat varies from fawn to reddish brown, with a dark stripe along the back, and numerous white spots on the back and flanks. The rump is pale, edged with black. The winter coat is drabber with only a faint indication of the white spots.

Length 130-160 cm, height 80-100 cm, weight: males 60-85 kg; females 30-50 kg.

Brief Encounter

In the late spring of 1991 I was lying on the ground in a young conifer plantation watching a pair of tree pipits feeding young, when I heard a slight disturbance to my right. I turned my head slowly and there, touchable, no more than a metre away was a doe with its small fawn looking down at me. We stared at each other motionless for a full 15 or 20 seconds. The deer displayed no sign of fear whatsoever, and then, without a sound, turned round and tiptoed silently away as if they did not want to disturb me. This was definitely one of the highlights of my wildlife watching experiences.

A male fallow deer in winter coat

In days gone by the **dormouse** *(Muscardinus avellanarius)* was a familiar animal to country folk. They were often kept as pets, as today's children keep hamsters. The secretive, nocturnal and rarely seen dormouse looks more like a small squirrel than a mouse, and is readily distinguished by its fluffy tail, orange-yellow fur and plump build. These mice are generally associated with bushes, particularly hazel, tall hedges, woodland edge and dense undergrowth.

Before the days of highly mechanised farming, they were regularly seen by farmworkers when laying hedges and cleaning ditches. Today, because of the loss of a large percentage of this kind of habitat, they are now considered rare; although it should be pointed out that because of their lifestyle they can easily be overlooked. Locally they are known to be present in the woodland edges on Beacon Hill, Trellech Hill and in the Gwent Wildlife Trust reserve at Croes Robert Wood, which is just out of the area between Trellech and Cwmcarvan, and where nest-boxes have been put up for them.

Dormice spend more of their time climbing in trees and bushes than other mice, and it is there they obtain most of their food. Their diet is mainly vegetarian, chiefly hazelnuts, beechmast, berries, buds, shoots and the occasional insect. The summer nests, usually well hidden in the undergrowth, are spherical, 10-15 cm in diameter with a 2 cm entrance hole. They are constructed out of the leaves of beech, oak, hazel or other trees, and these are skilfully woven together with an inner lining of bark fibre, often honeysuckle, grass and moss. A litter of three or four young is born in May, June or July; there is sometimes a second litter in August or September. The dormice also build a winter nest in a hole in the ground, between tree roots or some such similar place, and in October they roll themselves into a ball inside the nest and usually hibernate until the following spring. During hibernation their body temperature drops to that of the surroundings, and the heart and breathing rates are often reduced by 90 per cent or more. Length 6-9 cm, tail 5-7 cm, weight 15-25 gm.

The **wood mouse** *(Apodemus sylvaticus)* is probably the most widespread and abundant British mammal, and is sometimes known as the long-tailed field mouse. It has a brown back, the under-parts are greyish white, usually with a transition zone of yellowish fur and a yellow streak on its chest. It is not confined to woodlands, thriving equally well in fields, hedgerows, scrub and heathland. It is also abundant around gardens and farm buildings and often enters houses in the winter. Unlike house mice it does not smell. It moves very fast over the ground using long leaps of up to 80 cm, and it climbs and swims well. Seeds are the main food, along with shoots, buds, snails and a variety of insects. These mice dig their own burrow systems where they store food and have their young. Breeding starts in March and they can have four litters of four or five young each year. Length 8-11 cm, tail 7-11 cm, weight 14-22 gm.

The **yellow-necked mouse** *(Apodemus flavicollis)* resembles a large wood mouse with similar behaviour and lifestyle, but is distinguished by its distinct yellow collar and sandy brown coat. It is strictly nocturnal, characteristically having

Yellow-necked mouse at home in the branches

Right: A yellow necked mouse unusually feeding from a nut dispenser in broad daylight

large ears and eyes which are needed to pick up the slightest sound or movement. It is a good climber, often searching for food in the high branches. It is not as widespread as the wood mouse, being found mainly in the Welsh borders and the south-east of England. It likes to move into buildings in the winter. The diet of these mice consists mainly of seeds and fruit, such as acorns, hazel-nuts and blackberries, but they will also eat insects, snails and the eggs and nestlings of small birds when available. They have their four or five young in a nest of grass and leaves in an underground burrow. Length 8.8-13 cm, the tail is usually longer than the body 9-13.4 cm, weight 22-48 gm.

The Great Escape

Looking out of the window one morning in early spring, I was surprised to see a mouse feeding on a nut feeder hanging from a tree close to the house. On taking a closer look I realised it was a yellow-necked mouse. This made the activity even more unusual as these creatures are by nature strictly nocturnal, but it did highlight how flexible animals can be when the opportunity arises. The mouse fed on the nuts for several minutes then it scampered along the branch supporting the feeder, down the tree trunk and disappeared down a small hole on the terrace.

Over the next few days it appeared regularly at about the same time and I always knew when it was there as the birds would be queuing up to feed. On one occasion I was fortunate enough to see it appear at the hole on the terrace; it seemed very nervous, looking about, then darting back down the hole, then back out again before making a dash across to the tree, then up and along to the feeder.

Then, surprise, surprise, one day there were two mice on the feeder. By this time the birds were getting used to their presence, and the great tits and coal tits were starting to share the feeder with them. The comings and goings of the mice were always via the same well memorised route. I was watching them

feeding one day when suddenly they fled from the feeder in great panic. They raced back along their arboreal highway just as a black and white heat-seeking missile in the shape of a magpie came into view.

When the mice reached the tree trunk they did not run down it as before, but jumped off from a height of about two metres into a patch of adjacent ground elder. I couldn't see if they were holding paws, and I didn't hear any cries of 'Geronimo'! By now the magpie was very close behind and it crashed into the ground elder a split second behind them. It thrashed about in the herbage for a few seconds but to no avail. They had escaped.

One question I asked myself about this incident was how did the mice identify the threat, posed by a predator that was not part of their natural nocturnal environment? I did not know at the time that all would be revealed at a later date.

About a week after the great escape I had just refilled the nut feeder when one of the mice appeared at its exit hole on the terrace, but then darted back in. I had observed this nervous behaviour before so I decided to stand still and wait and see if it would re-appear. Sure enough, within a few seconds, it was out running across the terrace and up the tree. The feeder was at eye height to me and immediately the mouse was running along the branch towards me. Without hesitation it dropped down on to the feeder and started to feed. It was now less than an arm's length from me. From its relaxed behaviour it was obvious that this large stationary object, that had suddenly appeared on the scene, me, did not trigger any alarm bells. It seemed as though static objects posed no threat and could be ignored.

By this time it was eating with its back to me. I thought I would see if I could reach out and turn the feeder round so as to view the mouse head-on. This I did and the mouse appeared totally unperturbed. When I released the feeder, as it was under tension due to twisting, it started to spin gently clockwise and anti-clockwise. To my surprise the mouse just carried on feeding as if nothing was happening; maybe it enjoyed the carousel ride! I repeated the exercise several times, but the outcome was always the same. I was careful throughout to ensure it never saw my arm or hand moving.

I thought I would try the ultimate test, how would it respond if I touched it. So the next time it moved round the feeder and was positioned facing away from me, I reached out and touched it gently on its back. There was no reaction. Once again, I repeated this action several times, touching it on its back and tail in turn, but to my continued amazement it just carried on feeding.

By now it had occurred to me that movement must be the trigger to inducing a survival response. So the next time it faced me, I turned to move away, and the response was instantaneous. In a flash it raced back along the branch, and plunged into the safety of the ground elder.

Yellow-necked mice resemble large wood mice, with similar behaviour and life-style, but are distinguished by their distinct yellow collar and sandy brown coat. As I said, they are nocturnal, but there are always exceptions. Characteristically they have large ears and bulging convex eyes. Recent research has shown that the best-known site in England and Wales for this species is in Monmouthshire. This research has found that where they do occur, densities are low, except for rare hot-spots - such as the one near Usk which is the only one known currently in the U.K.

The **harvest mouse** (Micromys minutus) is one of our smallest mammals. They are active during both the day and night and as remarkably active climbers they can scale thin stems aided by a very flexible tail, which acts as a fifth limb. Less mobile than other mice on the ground, they inhabit hedges, young plantations, cornfields and other areas where there is long grass or weeds. Their status locally is difficult to assess: I personally have found only two old nests. Breeding takes place from April to September and there may be several litters, each with three to seven young. The young are reared in a nest built a few inches above ground, suspended in thick vegetation. The nests, not much larger than a tennis ball, are spherical and skillfully constructed from interwoven blades and stems of grass.

> I found a ball of grass among the hay
> And progged it as I passed and went away;
> And when I looked I fancied something stirred,
> And turned agen and hoped to catch the bird-
> When out an old mouse bolted in the wheats
> With all her young ones hanging at her teats;

From the poem *Mouse's Nest* by JOHN CLARE

Their diet consists of insects, seeds, fruit and buds. They are yellowish brown in colour with sharply separated whitish under-parts. Length 6-7.5 cm, tail 5-7 cm, weight 6-10 gm.

Unlike other mice the **house mouse** (Mus musculus), who's original home was probably the Asian steppes, has a strong smell. This smell taints the places where it lives, and is caused by the animal marking its territory with urine. These mice are widespread, living mostly in and around buildings, but they are extremely adaptable and can live anywhere. Some have even been found in frozen meat stores, where they had developed longer fur to protect them from the cold. They normally live close to their food source - and when it has gone they will move on. Their diet consists mainly of vegetable matter, but they have been known to eat unusual items, including soap. They gnaw to wear down their constantly growing front teeth and they have caused fires as a result of attacking electric cables.

Their nests are built in any secluded cavity, and made out of any soft material available. They are prolific breeders, having up to 10 litters a year, producing up to 50 young. The young are capable of breeding at six weeks old. They have a grey-brown greasy coat with a long scaly tail. Length 7.5-10.5 cm, tail 7-10 cm, weight 10-24 gm.

The **common shrew** (Sorex araneus) is, like all members of the shrew family, a small, short-legged mouse-like animal with a long pointed muzzle. Active day and night, the shrew is constantly on the move. Its food intake is enormous, as it needs to eat between half to three-quarters of its own weight daily, and will starve if it goes without food for more than about three hours. As a shrew's vision is poor, it finds food with the aid of long tactile hairs on the muzzle, coupled to good hearing. Undemanding in its choice of habitat, it can be found practically everywhere there is low ground-covering vegetation.

A shrew's diet consists of insects, larvae, earthworms, woodlice and other small invertebrates, fresh carrion and seeds. It builds its nest either below ground, or just on the surface but well hidden in the undergrowth. A female may produce three or more litters of five to eight young a year. These mice are brownish black on the back and sides with paler under-parts. They emit two types of sound: a subdued twittering and a high-pitched aggressive squeak, which is why the term 'shrewish' is often applied to a scolding woman. Cats often kill but rarely eat them, and this is probably due to their musky smell. Length 7-9 cm, tail is a relatively short 3.5-4.5 cm, weight 3.5-14 gm.

The **pygmy shrew** (*Sorex minutus*) is Britain's smallest mammal. It is so small that it is near the limit at which a warm-blooded animal can survive. If it were any smaller its body surface would be too great for its bulk and it would lose heat too rapidly to be able to maintain a warm body temperature. Though scarcer, its habits and habitat requirements are similar to the common shrew. It is uniform brown in colour. Length 4.3-6 cm, tail 3-4.6 cm, weight 2.5-6.0 gm.

As its name suggests, the **water shrew** (*Neomys fodiens*) tends to be found in damp places where they prey on worms, insect larvae and spiders, but can be found some distance from water, and even in woodland. They will take to water, hunting in ponds and streams for small fish, tadpoles and even quite large frogs. A poisonous salivary gland secretion kills their prey. Like all shrews, they are active day or night, eating roughly their own weight daily. The compact nest of moss and leaves is usually built underground, just below the surface, where

A rarely seen water shrew

two or three litters of three to eight young are reared yearly. As with all shrews their numbers are prone to large fluctuations. They have a black coat and silvery white under-parts with white eyebrows and ear tips. Length 7-9.6 cm, tail 4.7-7.7 cm, weight 10.0-23.0 gm.

The ubiquitous **brown rat** (*Rattus norvegicus*) is a widespread pest and carrier of disease. They are mainly associated with inhabited areas but do move out into more open country in the summer months. Originally native to south and east Asia, they are thought to have spread to Britain in the early 18th century, partly by their own migration and partly aboard ships. They are now a worldwide pest. They will eat almost anything and thrive where there are food stores or waste, so farmyards are particularly prone to invasion. They are mostly active at night, particularly at dusk and early in the morning. If they are seen during the day, it is usually due to hunger or disturbance.

They are very wary and suspicious of any change in their immediate surroundings. Where food and shelter are readily available, they can breed throughout the year, making a nest in a cavity of loose straw, rags or similar material, and a female can produce up to five litters of six to ten young, which in turn can breed after three months. The nest is built underground when living outdoors. The brown rat has coarse grey-brown fur, small finely haired ears and a thick, scaly tail; the white laboratory rat is an albino form. Length 21-27 cm, tail 17.0-23.0 cm, weight up to 500 gm.

The **field vole** *(Microtus agrestis)*, or short-tailed vole, is common throughout the area, living in hedgerows, rough grassland in the damp tussocks, woodland edges and young tree plantations. Aggressive and noisy, field voles utter squeaks and angry chattering noises as they defend their territories. Conspicuous runways among the grass stems visually advertise their presence; these are usually centred on their nest site.

Their diet consists mainly of grass, particularly the succulent lower stems; they will also eat bulbs, roots and tree bark at ground level. Their nest may be below or above ground, but, in the latter case, it is always well hidden, either in the vegetation or under a fallen branch or similar object. They are prolific breeders producing four to five litters of four to six young yearly, but their population increases and decreases over a three to five year cycle. Field voles have many enemies, and provide an important source of food for nearly all the avian and mammalian predators here. They are the main food of barn owls, forming 90 per cent of their diet. Their colour varies from ochre to deep brown, with grey under-parts, a blunt nose and short ears. Length 9.5-13.5 cm, tail 2.7-4.6 cm, weight 19.0-52 gm.

The **bank vole** *(Clethrionomys glareolus)* is about the same size as the field vole but has a glossy chestnut-brown coat and creamy grey under-parts with more prominent ears. It is most active at dusk and dawn, but it is not a particularly retiring species and providing there is plenty of cover it will move about in the day. Although it may sometimes be found in wet grass, it much prefers to live where there is dense cover and is rarely found far from bramble thickets or hedgerows. It is common in country gardens. It runs fast over the ground and climbs with great agility, ascending to considerable heights in trees. Seeds, berries, nuts, green plants, insects and fungi are all part of its diet. The breeding nest, which is made of grass and leaves, is sometimes built above ground in a tree stump, or under a boulder, but is usually below ground. They have four to five litters of three to six young yearly. Length 8-12.5 cm, tail 3.6-7.2 cm, weight 16-30 gm.

The **mole** *(Talpa europaea)*, which is related to the hedgehog, spends the greater part of its solitary life underground in an extensive, branched system of burrows. Usually only one mole lives in each system. These burrows can vary in depth from five to 100 cm, but are usually found at a depth of between 10 and 20 cm. Moles dig the earth with their heavily clawed forelimbs, scraping it backwards with the hind limbs. When a suitable amount of earth has been loosened, the mole turns and pushes the soil back through the burrow and up through an oblique hole to the surface, thereby forming a molehill. It is strong enough to be able to move twice its own weight of soil in a minute.

Moles come to the surface to collect grass and leaves to make a nest, and to look for food when the ground is very dry. They feed mainly on earthworms, beetles and snails, but if the opportunity arises, they will also take small frogs and mice.

Moles are common where the soil is loose and easy to dig. They have many predators. Foxes and badgers dig up their nests, weasels hunt them in their burrows, and many young moles are taken by birds of prey. Gardeners and farmers dislike them as molehills spoil lawns and sports grounds, and disturb the roots of crops. Molehills are a hazard for livestock, particularly horses, and cause damage to the blades of cutting machines. As late as the 1950s moles were trapped for their fur, which was used for hat and coat trimmings.

This black or slate-grey fur, which is very dense, silky-soft and impenetrable, stands out at right angles from the body and does not lie in any one direction. This allows a mole to move with ease in either direction in its burrow. Its vision is poor and it can probably only differentiate between light and dark, but a mole's senses of touch and smell at short range are highly developed.

The female builds a nest of grass and leaves and usually a single litter of two to six young is born between April and June. The young become independent at four to five weeks. Length 11.5-15 cm, tail 2-3.4 cm, weight 65-120 gm.

The **rabbit** (*Oryctolagus cuniculus*) was originally native to the Mediterranean area and was introduced into Britain from Europe in the 12th century. As a valuable source of meat and skins, the rabbit was for hundreds of years protected by landowners, with poaching severely punished. For a long period, they remained a profitable part of the rural economy, but in the last 200 years they have became the most familiar wild animal of the British countryside, and one of the most destructive agricultural pests, with the result that they are now subject to pest control.

A sociable animal, the rabbit lives in colonies or warrens where a strict hierarchy is maintained. The warrens are usually a complicated series of burrows dug in the earth with several entrances, but rabbits are also known to live above ground in dense undergrowth or in rocky terrain. The myxomatosis epidemic which broke out in Britain in 1954 almost wiped out the rabbit population of an estimated 60 million. Following their demise, the improvement in crop production and vegetation growth was very noticeable.

Although the disease, which is transmitted by any biting or bloodsucking insect such as a flea or a mosquito, still breaks out periodically, there are indications that many rabbits are immune. Locally rabbits do appear to be on the increase. Breeding may occur throughout the year, but in general takes place between January and June. On average a doe produces about 10 live young a year which are sexually active within three months. The young are born below ground in a prepared nest, which is usually made at the end of a specially dug burrow; this is then lined with hay and fur from the doe's pelt. This nesting burrow is up to one metre long and the entrance is blocked with earth whenever the doe leaves the young.

The rabbit's coat is generally greyish brown with an area of orange-coloured hair at the nape of its neck, the under-parts are white, and the short tail is black on top and white underneath. Completely black specimens occur occasionally. Food consists of all kinds of plant matter of which grass plays the most important role during the summer. Rabbits cause a great deal of damage to various field crops, vegetables and trees by nibbling shoots and gnawing bark. The daily food requirement is about 0.5 kg. Length 34-45 cm, tail 4.0-8.0 cm, weight 1.3-2.2 kg.

The **hedgehog** (*Erinaceus europaeus*) is that prickly creature of the fields, gardens and hedgerows, and fairly common in this district, but its numbers do seem to have declined in recent years. It lies hidden during the day, coming out at night to hunt for food, which it finds by rooting about amongst fallen leaves, snuffling and snorting loudly as it searches. It is most active at dusk and dawn. Hedgehogs feed mainly on worms, insects and snails, but will also eat fruit, frogs, reptiles and the eggs and nestlings of ground-nesting birds. Mating takes place in April and May shortly after they come out of hibernation. The three to seven young, which are fully grown at three months, are born in a well-lined nest on the ground, well hidden under a pile of brushwood or in a compost heap. They may have a second litter in late summer.

Hedgehogs hibernate between October and April in a large nest of grass, leaves and moss. Their natural enemies are foxes and badgers, whose high population locally may account for hedgehogs' declining numbers. Many are killed on the roads, where their natural response to hearing an approaching car is to curl up instantly into a ball, with the resulting fatal consequence. As many dog owners will know from experience, after their pet has had contact with one, hedgehogs are generally flea ridden. Their spines are about 2 cm long; they are dark brown or black in colour, with white ends. The head and under-parts are covered with long, stiff, yellowish white hair, they have small eyes and ears and short tails. Some specimens are very pale, and albinos have been seen. Length 23-30 cm, tail 2.5 cm, weight 450-1200 gm.

A mole taking a quick look at the outside world

Chapter 8
The bats

Many people dislike bats, but they are harmless and very interesting creatures. They are furry, social, flying mammals that spend hours each day grooming themselves. They are the only mammals capable of flying long distances, using a modified form of the limbs common to all mammals. Their wings are a membrane of skin supported by arms and elongated fingers. The first finger is short and equipped with a claw. Mating occurs in autumn or winter, but with delayed fertilisation, the young are not born until June or July. The baby is suckled frequently day and night; in general, it can fly after three weeks and is weaned after five.

As they have poorly developed hind limbs bats do not walk far. They track down their prey by means of an elaborate echo-location system similar to the radar scanning equipment used in ships and aeroplanes. Horseshoe bats emit sound through their nostrils, which is focused via a fleshy cone-shaped trumpet on their snout. Ordinary bats emit sound through their mouth and have in each ear a fleshy spike known as a tragus, which is part of their sound reception system.

Unlike most other mammals they do not have a steady body temperature. In flight, they have a body temperature of 42 degrees centigrade, coupled with a pulse rate of 1000 per minute. On landing, their temperature rapidly falls 10 degrees centigrade for digestion and later falls to the surrounding ambient temperature. Bats can live up to 30 years.

Under the Wildlife and Countryside Act it is illegal for anyone without a licence intentionally to kill, injure or handle a wild bat of any species; or to possess a bat, whether live or dead; or to disturb a bat when roosting.

The **lesser horseshoe bat** *(Rhinolophus hipposideros)* is a member of the horseshoe bat family, which have a characteristic leaf-like outgrowth of skin - known as nose leaves - around the muzzle. These nose-leaves are used to direct the high-pitched sounds the bat emits to navigate and hunt its prey. Probably scarce locally, this particular bat was originally associated with caves, but has adapted to human habitation. It likes to hibernate in damp cellars and caves from late September to May, but they can be seen in the summer months hanging from the ceilings or beams inside farm buildings. Ten to fifteen of them regularly appear in a farm building on Beacon Hill in the summer, but do not hibernate there. In the resting position the bat normally hangs free, not in a crevice, head downward, suspended by its feet with its wings wrapped around its body like a cloak. Because of its rounded body it finds crawling difficult, so it needs a roost to which it can fly direct.

Its diet consists of moths, flies, small beetles, spiders and early hibernating butterflies seeking refuge in the same buildings, as proven by the numerous wings found scattered like confetti on the floor. The female usually produces a single offspring in June or July, which she suckles; the young take to the wing after about three weeks, and are independent after about eight weeks. It is one of Europe's smallest types of bat. Length 3.7-4 cm, wingspan of 20-25 cm, weight 3-9 gm.

The characteristic horseshoe-shaped nose leaves and the clawed first fingers of the lesser horseshoe bat

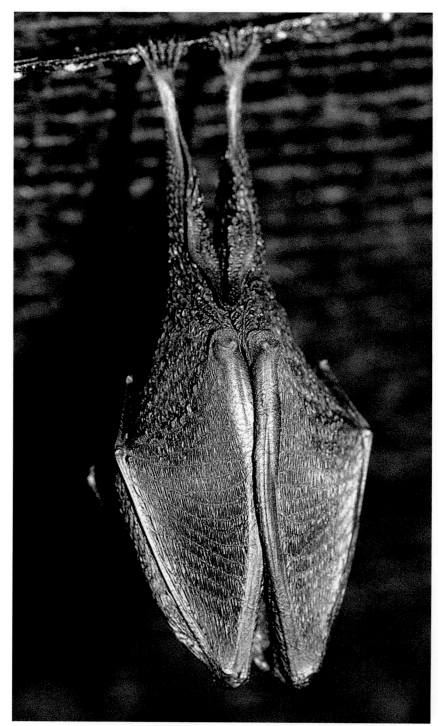

Lesser horseshoe bat at rest within its hibernaculum

The tiny **pipistrelle bat** *(Pipistrellus pipistrellus)* is our smallest bat, and the most common here, regularly seen flying along woodland rides and edges. These bats can be found roosting in the summer in the roof space of buildings, under the roof tiles, behind fascia boards, behind loose bark on trees and in any similar confined space. They will also take to specially constructed nest-boxes. Their winter quarters are similar, but some do hibernate in caves.

They can be seen foraging for insects, 15 to 30 minutes before sunset. Their flight is fast and fluttery with frequent twists and dives as they chase their prey. They can occasionally also be seen in broad daylight. Their diet consists mainly of small flies, gnats and moths. Warmth is essential to the tiny young, which are usually born in June. They are hairless for a week after birth, and consequently are very vulnerable to the cold, but they become independent in about two months. Hibernation is normally from late October to March, but may be interrupted. They vary in colour from orange-brown to pale grey-brown. Length 3.3-5.2 cm, wingspan 18-22 cm, weight 3.8-7 gm.

The **noctule bat** *(Nyctalus noctula)* is Britain's largest bat, with a wingspan up to 40 cm. I would consider this bat rare here as I have only seen it on a handful of occasions. The high-flying noctule bat is often on the wing before dark, and once I saw one swooping after insects in the company of a party of house martins and swifts. They are mostly tree dwellers, roosting in hollow trees or old woodpecker nests, and only on rare occasions will they take up residence in a building. The breeding cycle and hibernation pattern are similar to other bats. Their diet consists of large insects such as moths and cockchafer beetles. The noctule is a sturdily built species with long, narrow wings, a broad head with wide-set ears. Its back is covered with golden-brown fur, and the under-parts are slightly paler. Length 7-8 cm, wingspan

37-41 cm, weight 20-35 gm.

The **long-eared bat** *(Plecotus auritus)* is fairly common here, and is principally a woodland species, but it has adapted to living and breeding in buildings. These bats emerge to hunt for food at twilight, gliding around the trees and low vegetation. The long-eared bat's huge ears, which are 3-4.2 cm long, are part of a system of echo-location. This is not only sensitive enough to detect flying insects, but also to locate them resting on foliage.

In flight these bats are slow and fluttering, as they hover to take insects or larvae direct from the foliage. They sometimes land on tree stumps, or on the ground to forage for food. During flight their ears are directed forwards, and the body is held somewhat obliquely in the air, giving it a characteristic flight silhouette. Diet consists of moths, butterflies, gnats, craneflies and other insects; larger prey is often eaten at fixed feeding places.

Long-eared bats usually hibernate alone from November to March, hanging from the roof or walls, or in crevices. The breeding cycle is similar to other bats. The bat has broad wings; its body is covered with light brown fur which is slightly paler underneath. Length 4-5 cm, wingspan 25 cm, weight 5-10 gm.

The **Natterer's bat** *(Myotis nattereri)* is named after its discoverer, an early 19th century Austrian naturalist. It tends to emerge at sunset, flying low along woodland rides or across the treetops. Its flight is slow and steady, without any of the rapid changes in direction that are the accepted hallmark of flying bats. Its diet consists mainly of various flying insects, but not all prey is taken on the wing and some insects are picked from the foliage. The sexes are segregated, with the males living solitarily. In the summer breeding colonies of females gather in hollow trees or in roof spaces of buildings. Females bear only one young in June or July, and these can fly in August.

They hibernate from December to March in hollow trees, caves or buildings. They are scarce locally. They have long drooping ears and their upper-parts are covered with grey-brown fur which has a reddish sheen, while the under-parts are white. The colour is a distinctive aid to identification when on the wing. Length 4-5 cm, wingspan 25-28 cm, weight 5-10 gm.

Chapter 9
Reptiles and amphibians

The **common lizard** (*Lacerta vivipara*), sometimes called the viviparous lizard, can be seen locally in the young forest plantations, hedgerows, rough grassland, or any grass or scrub covered bank. These lizards can often be found basking in the spring on a warm surface such as a tree stump or a stone, especially in the morning and afternoon.

They emerge from hibernation in early spring, and initially bask a great deal, but as the weather gets warmer, they do not have to bask as much. When disturbed they will dart into hiding, but once disturbance stops are quick to reappear.

Lizards feed mainly on earthworms, insects and larvae, but they will eat anything living of a suitable size, even occasionally eating the young of their own species. Large victims are shaken and banged on the ground, and then swallowed whole, irrespective of size. The prey is never bitten.

Mating takes place in April or May, and the live young are born nearly three months later. Before the birth the female finds a sheltered place amongst the herbage and usually produces six to eight young. The young lizards are born fully formed within a transparent membrane that breaks immediately. When the birth is completed, the female has nothing more to do with the young, which are black and 30-38 mm long, and can run about almost immediately, looking for food. Lizards slough at intervals of two to three months when they are not hibernating. When pursued, they can run very fast. If caught by the tail, they can break it off (autotomy) leaving the amputated section still wriggling. This often allows the lizard to escape, and a new tail grows out from the breakage point.

The common lizard has many enemies, including foxes, crows and birds of prey. Its colour can vary, but is generally grey to brown, with rows of paler spots along its back. In the male, the under-parts are yellow-orange, with small black spots, whereas the female is a yellow-white without the spots. Length 10-16 cm, tail 5-8 cm.

Young common lizards hunting for food

Right: Common Lizard on a drystone wall basking in the late evening sun

The **slow-worm** *(Anguis fragilis)* or blindworm is often mistaken for a snake, but although legless, it is a lizard. The long cylindrical snake-like body is the same thickness throughout; it passes without any constriction into a small head with a rounded snout. Although fairly common, it is rarely seen. It is essentially a terrestrial animal, which lives in damp, shady places, under stones or in burrows, which it digs with its snout. They can also be found in woodland, fields and gardens. Slow-worms like to bask in partial sunlight, but not in the open. They can often be found on a warm day under corrugated sheeting or any similar object that has been left lying on the ground.

Hibernation underground begins in October and ends in March or April when mating takes place. The young are usually born below ground in late August or early September. The ovoviviparous young - between 5 and 20 - are each born in a transparent, yellow egg membrane, from which they quickly break out. At birth the young are 6-9 cm long and are active immediately, able to find and eat small worms and slugs. This is their main diet, but insects and spiders are also taken. They will only eat live prey - and, as slug eaters, they are a great asset to any garden. Hedgehogs, adders, birds of prey and, occasionally, toads prey on them. They can live longer than any other lizard, with some surviving over 50 years in captivity, but such an age is unlikely in the wild. Like other lizards, they have the protective action of autotomy. If seized by the tail, they break it off by contraction of the muscles; this fracture occurs across the vertebrae, not between them. They then have the ability to grow a new tail, which can be identified by its stumpy appearance. Slow-worms vary in colour from grey to light, dark or coppery brown; the females have dark brown flanks, sometimes with a dark stripe. The males are more uniform in colour. Length up to 50 cm, just over half of which is tail.

The **adder** *(Vipera berus)* is the most common British snake and the only poisonous one. It is dangerous to humans, but rarely is its bite fatal; even so, treatment should always be sought as soon as possible. Adders are very timid, and normally slither away before anyone gets close enough to be bitten. These snakes live in almost any dry place, but prefer open areas like heath and moorland. Locally they are most likely to be seen in the newly planted plantations, and on the edge of forest rides.

They emerge from hibernation in March or April and can be found basking in the early morning sun, on a tree stump or other warm surface. They prefer gentle warmth to the strong heat of the midday sun.

A good local site for viewing adders is just outside the R.S.P.B. office at Nags Head in the Forest of Dean, where, on a spring morning, numerous adders and an occasional grass snake can be seen basking on piles of provisioned grass cuttings. Mating usually takes place in April and up to 15 young are born in August to September, and are capable of feeding themselves. They take three to four years to reach maturity. Adders shed their skins from time to time, the cast-off skin advertising their presence. They go into hibernation in holes or under tree stumps in October when the nights become cold.

A sunbathing adder

Right: Basking slow worm

Nature in the Raw

It was a bright sunny morning in late May when I set out for a walk through the local woods. The air was vibrant with the sound of birdsong and buzzing bees. The good early spring weather meant the trees were in full leaf, presenting a wonderful tapestry of shades of green.

I had just stepped out of the sunlight on to a forest track blanketed in shadow, when I spotted a pair of extremely agitated coal tits. The birds, with their beaks full of caterpillars, were fluttering about in the lower branches of a Scots pine uttering incessant alarm calls. At first, I thought it was my presence beside their hitherto undisclosed nest that was upsetting them. But past experience told me that coal tits soon accept people being there, and normally carry on feeding their young. So what was the cause of their concern?

Suddenly I noticed a movement in a tuft of grass at the base of the tree. A closer inspection revealed a female adder trying to ingest a struggling fledgling. As I approached closer the adder became aware of my presence, released the fledgling, which now appeared to be dead, and slithered into a nearby hole. The hole, presumably the coal tits' nest, went underneath some exposed tree roots. I peered into the hole and could just make out the snake, which started hissing at me. In the meantime, the coal tits fluttered about overhead keeping up their incessant calling, partly drowning the singing of a neighbouring redstart and blackcap, who appeared unconcerned with the life and death struggle I had witnessed. Realising there was little I could do, I continued my walk, making a mental note to return the same way.

On my return about an hour later, the coal tits were still alarmed. An inspection of the nest site showed that the dead fledgling had gone, and as tapping of the surrounding tree roots prompted no response, I assumed the adder had gone too. As I turned to walk away, I heard a hissing sound and there, not more than a few metres away camouflaged against a backcloth of pine needles, was the female adder. I withdrew, thinking that if there were any survivors in the nest, the snake should be removed from the nest site in the hope that this would prevent any further predation. I found a small twiggy coniferous branch and scooped up the adder. After I had carried it for about 20 metres it wriggled free and fell to the ground, and immediately regurgitated two three-quarter grown coal tit fledglings and an egg, presumably infertile. I quickly scooped up the adder again and carried it a further 200 metres away from the nest site, placed it on the ground and watched it slither away into the safety of the undergrowth. I returned to the nest site to find that the coal tits were feeding the survivor(s).

Out of curiosity, I visited the nest site the following day and to my dismay I found a fox had dug it out, and there was no sign of the coal tits. Returning home, I reflected on the events of the past couple of days with mixed feelings. I had been privileged to witness at first hand this cruel, rarely seen struggle for survival, but felt sorry for the coal tits, which had seemed destined to lose their brood.

I pondered the regurgitation of the fledglings by the adder when it was dropped, and wondered if it was some form of innate survival or distraction mechanism. Did the snake regurgitate the food to preoccupy her adversary and enable escape, or was it the shock of the fall that caused her to do so?

Young adder basking

Adders feed on lizards, small rodents, frogs, toads and the nestlings of ground nesting birds; they do not feed every day, as a large meal may last a week. Apart from man, their natural enemies are crows, birds of prey, and surprisingly, hedgehogs. Their most distinctive features are a dark zigzag line along the back and a V mark behind the head. The males are silvery grey or yellowy green, and measure up to 60 cm; the females are usually duller and browner and can measure up to 76 cm.

The **grass snake** *(Natrix natrix)* is a lover of damp ditches, pond banks and the edges of streams. Harmless to humans, they feed mainly on frogs and small newts, which they catch on land or in the water, as they are good swimmers. They will also eat the eggs and nestlings of ground-nesting birds. They come out of hibernation in April and mating takes place in May or June; the female lays her 10-30 eggs in July. The grass snake is the only British snake to lay its eggs in a place where heat is generated, such as a midden or compost heap. On hatching the young can immediately fend for themselves, eating slugs and earthworms.

Like all reptiles grass snakes spend a lot of time basking, usually near undergrowth so they can rapidly retreat if disturbed.

During October they leave their damp summer abodes and go into hibernation in stone walls or under tree roots. Grass snakes have many enemies; the eggs are taken by rats, stoats and other small mammals, which also feed on the newly hatched young. They can be identified by two yellow crescent-shaped patches on the nape of the neck, coupled to two black triangles. The upper-parts are olive or grey-green, and the flanks are usually marked with black bars. The throat and the front part of the underside are whitish; the belly is patterned with white, grey and black. The eye has a rounded pupil, unlike the adder, which has a slit-shaped one. Length: female snakes can grow up to 2 m, males are smaller.

Open wooded areas, moist pastures, and gardens not too far from water are the favoured habitat of the **common frog** *(Rana temporaria)*. In autumn, from

Common frog on the look out for a tasty morsel

about mid-October, they hibernate in sheltered places on land or in the muddy bottoms of ponds. They emerge to move to breeding ponds in February or March, and it is not unusual to find a hundred or more using a pond for spawning. Egg laying goes on from March to April. Ordinarily frogs make no sound, but a purring, croaking call can be heard in the breeding season, and this croaking can be heard from some distance if a number of frogs are involved. The egg (spawn) is laid in a transparent jelly that protects the embryo frog. A female can produce up to 3000 eggs. After spawning the frogs stay in the water until the weather gets warmer, then leave to live on land. Depending on the temperature the tadpoles hatch from the eggs after 14 days or more. After three months they have developed four legs, ready for life on land.

When frogs leave the pond, birds and other predators eat them in large numbers. Frogs of all ages have many natural enemies, for they are eaten by hedgehogs, rats, foxes, grass snakes, crows and herons, to name a few. As frogs eat insects, slugs and snails, they are good friends to the gardener.

A young grass snake basking

The body colour of the common frog varies widely from dark greenish grey to chestnut or yellow, but all have a distinctive dark patch behind the eye with dark bars on the limbs. They move by hopping and leaping; they do not crawl. When on land they breathe through their nostrils, but they also absorb oxygen through the skin, and during hibernation this is their sole means of respiration. Length 7-9 cm.

The **common toad** (*Bufo bufo*) migration in March or early April can be a spectacular affair. Within the space of a few days, large numbers of toads leave hibernation, and head for their breeding pond, climbing over obstacles and crossing roads in a mass. Vehicles kill many, and in some places warning signs are put up on busy roads. There is a minor road crossing point near Five Trees at the northern edge of the area, where this phenomenon can be witnessed.

Toads like to spawn in deep water where the female lays a two to three metre long jelly-like string of up to 7000 eggs, which become entangled in the plant life of the pond. The eggs develop into tadpoles, and then grow into young toads over a three to four month period, depending on the temperature. Like the young frogs, they have the same group of natural enemies, and only five per cent survive to maturity. But they can live up to 20 years. When spawning is completed the adults leave the pond to live alone through the summer, where most of the time is spent sheltering under stones, tree roots or in among dense vegetation, emerging at night to feed. Unlike frogs, toads walk as described by Norman MacCaig:

> *Stop looking like a purse. How could a purse*
> *squeeze under the rickety door and sit,*
> *full of satisfaction, in a man's house?*
>
> *You clamber towards me on your four corners-*
> *Right hand, left foot, left hand, right foot.*

From the poem *Toad* by Norman MacCaig

Their diet consists of worms, slugs, woodlice, insects and larvae, making them very beneficial in the garden.

They sit and wait for their prey, seizing it with their long sticky tongue, which is rooted at the front of the mouth and can be extended up to one centimetre. The toad is broad and plump, with a short head. It has a dry warty skin, the back may be brownish black, grey-brown or olive, and the underside is greyish. Length: female up to 10 cm, male up to 7 cm.

The **smooth newt** (*Triturus vulgaris*) is the most common British newt. They can be found in open woodland, wet pastures or gardens, provided there are suitable ponds or water nearby for breeding. The breeding season starts in early spring and will take place in any standing water, including ditches. The females produce 200-300 single eggs, which are laid on water plant leaves, each enclosed in a protective jelly coat. Like those of frogs and toads, the eggs hatch into a larval stage similar to that of a tadpole, which has gills. In 10 weeks lungs and limbs have grown, the gills go and the young newt, an eft, leaves the water.

After the breeding season the adults move on to the land, hiding under stones, logs or in thick grass. They emerge at night to hunt for slugs, worms and insects. All newts shed their skin, a process known as sloughing. In spring this may happen weekly. In winter they hibernate under moss or any object that will protect them from the frost. Outside of the breeding season the skin is slightly warty and rather like velvet, but after the newt enters the water in spring it becomes smooth. During the breeding season the male - which is brown to olive brown in colour and marked with darker spots - develops a high crest along its back and tail, and the pale yellow under-parts turn a bright orange. This crest is later reabsorbed when the breeding season is over. The female is usually a paler grey-yellow or brown. Length 7-10 cm. The male is larger than the female.

The **palmate newt** (*Triturus helveticus*) can be found in the small ponds in the locality. It usually emerges from its winter quarters in March to April, moving straight to water to breed. Over a period of 3-4 weeks the female lays 300-400 eggs. These are attached singly to aquatic plants. The newly hatched larvae are 8mm long and when metamorphosis is complete they measure 25 mm. Palmate

The patient nocturnal toad

Male great crested newt on route to a breeding pond

voraciously on water fleas and fly larvae. Metamorphosis is complete by September when they leave the water. By this time the larvae are up to eight cm long, and have lost their gills and acquired functional lungs. The young winter under moss, tree roots or a hole in the ground, and become sexually mature after two years.

The skin of the great crested newt is very warty with numerous mucous glands; some of these produce a secretion that has an irritating and possibly lethal action on predators. These newts feed on worms, snails and larvae, and the prey is usually shaken violently before being swallowed. The male has a deeply toothed dorsal crest; the upper parts are dark brown or black with small white spots down the sides. The under-parts are yellow or orange spotted or marbled with black. The female, which is larger, is similar in colour but lacks the crest. Length 12-16 cm.

newts feed mainly on small worms, insects and their larvae. The upper-parts of the male are olive-green or olive-brown with small dark spots. The underside is pale orange or yellow, usually uniformly coloured, but sometimes there are spots. In the breeding season the male has a low dorsal crest which increases slightly on the tail. The colour of the female is similar to the smooth newt. In all cases the body is slender and smooth to touch. Length 8-9cm, the female can be slightly longer.

The **great crested newt** (*Triturus cristatus*) is the largest British newt, but sadly it is in decline. It is still to be found in the ponds close to Trellech. Unlike the smooth newt, it prefers deep water, and, after breeding, some adults remain in the water until the autumn, and will even hibernate in the mud at the bottom of the pond. But the majority hibernate on land.

Egg laying begins in April or May, with the 200-300 eggs being laid singly and attached to the underside of a small leaf of a pond plant, which is curled round it. The larvae hatch after two to three weeks, proceeding to feed

Part Three

Insects

The word insect means 'in sections'. An insect's body is in three parts - the head, thorax and abdomen. On the thorax are three pairs of jointed legs. Some relatives of insects - not true insects but often confused with them - are the spiders, centipedes and woodlice. They have similar jointed legs, but usually more of them.

Insects are the most successful class of animals on earth, in terms of their numbers of species and also the total number of each individual species. They exploit almost every nook and cranny of the earth's surface. They are fast and prolific breeders, and some have even dispensed with the sexes, reproducing by virgin birth, or parthenogenesis.

In Britain's temperate climate it is during the spring and summer that the insects are generally active - mating, egg laying and feeding. Winter is the time of hibernation. Some species winter in the adult state (imago) as the appearance of peacock and tortoiseshell butterflies in the dark corners of the garden shed or outbuildings will testify. Others pass the winter in the larval form in some sheltered spot, and some in the chrysalis or pupal state, lying dormant until the spring, when the imago appears. Some insects - including certain butterflies and moths - lay their eggs in the autumn, and these do not hatch until the warm spring sun has triggered the host food plants to grow.

There are more than 20,000 species of insects in Britain. Although they are not all found locally, a large number are here, and any attempt to locate and identify them all would be a few lifetimes' work.

The majority of our native insects are small, passing unnoticed unless deliberately sought out. Others, although larger, are equally difficult to find, hidden in the soil, or cleverly camouflaged on tree trunks and among living or decaying vegetation. A significant number, however, can be seen, generally attracting our attention by their bright colours or their movement. The following presents some of the more colourful and interesting ones.

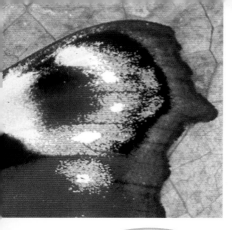

Chapter 10
Butterflies and moths

Pieridae Family

Two butterflies to be seen early in the year are the **brimstone** *(Gonepteryx rhamni)* and the **orange-tip** *(Anthocharis cardamines)*. Both are members of the Pieridae family. The brimstone is the large butterfly we see earliest in the year, suggesting spring is just around the corner. It is aptly named; for the male is bright yellow - the original 'butter fly' - the female is a greenish white.

The adults hibernate but may be seen flying as early as February on a mild day. The orange-tip is a medium-small butterfly, fairly common here, which is seen on the wing in May and June. It favours damp places and woodland edges, where its main food plants are garlic mustard and the cuckoo flower, the seedpod of which looks like a resting caterpillar. The males have the distinctive orange wing tip, edged with black; the females lack the orange.

The next two butterflies, also members of the pieridae family, need no description, particularly to those readers who grow their own vegetables. They are the **large white** *(Pieris brassicae)* and the **small white** *(Pieris rapae)*, and the popular name for both is 'cabbage white'. The caterpillars of both species are notorious for the damage they do to cabbage and allied garden plants. The caterpillars of the large white are conspicuous and feed on the outer leaves, whereas the small white caterpillars feed hidden in the cabbage heart. A further member of this family is the **clouded yellow** *(Colias croceus)* a well known but unpredictable migrant that arrives here from southern Europe. The male is a distinctive marigold yellow with black borders to its wings; the black border is punctuated with yellow spots in the case of the female. It has been seen on occasions in Fedw Fawr and in 2004 was seen in Gwent Wildlife Trusts New Grove Meadows Nature Reserve.

Orange tip butterfly warming up on cat's-ear

Right: Female brimstone butterfly feeding on escallonia blossom

Nymphalidae family

Next, we come to the largest and most beautiful butterflies to be seen in the countryside and identified by the early entomologists as the aristocrats. Together with the fritillaries they make up the family called the Nymphalidae. They fully live up to the late Dame Miriam Rothschild's wonderfully evocative description of *'dream flowers which have broken loose from their stalks and escaped into the sunshine'*. The highly mobile **peacock** *(Inachis io)*, with a wingspan of up to 7 cm, is a conspicuous, familiar and unmistakable visitor to our gardens. Along with its close relations the equally mobile **small tortoiseshell** *(Aglais urticae)* and **red admiral** *(Vanessa atalanta)*, it can regularly be seen feeding on the flowers of buddleia shrubs, field and hedgerow thistles, and, later in the year, ivy blossom is a favoured source of nectar.

Red admiral feeding on valerian

I'll see again the green leaves suddenly
Turned into flowers by resting butterflies;
While all around are small, brown, working bees,
And hairy black-and-ambers, twice their size.

From the poem *The Song of Life* by W.H. DAVIES

The caterpillars of all three species feed on nettles, so we should all try and keep an untidy corner for them in our gardens. Also belonging to the same group are the **painted lady** *(Cynthia cardui)* and the solitary **comma** *(Polygonia c-album)*.

The latter is fairly rare, but can be recognised by the ragged outline of its wings, which at first glance give it the look of a damaged small tortoiseshell. It is a master of disguise; when at rest the cryptic underwing colouring together with the broken outline, gives it an appearance of a dead leaf. The superb camouflage enhances its chances of survival during hibernation. It derives its name from the white 'comma mark' on the underside of its wing.

Small tortoiseshell butterfly warming up in the sun

Right: The beautiful peacock butterfly warming up on a dock leaf

Resting comma butterfly showing the comma mark on the underside of its wing

The painted lady is a powerful flying migrant that comes to Britain in May or June from south-west Europe and North Africa. Consequently, their numbers vary from year to year; in 1997 and 2002 there were large influxes. Some of the early migrants do lay eggs, giving rise to a second generation of butterflies in September and October, but unfortunately, they cannot survive the damp and cold of a British winter.

A woodland member of this group that has not been seen here since 1992 and one that is in decline nationally is the **pearl-bordered fritillary** *(Boloria euphrosyne)*. Once it was quite common in the county along sunny open woodland rides and clearings, where its host food plant dog violet grows. It would be exciting to discover that a small colony still existed somewhere locally. It gets its name from the seven pearls or small white spots that border the underside margins of the rear wings.

Lastly, an uncommon member of this group, which can also be seen locally, is the graceful, woodland-dwelling **white admiral** *(Limenitis camilla)*. This is a species that has been expanding its range in recent years, and I have seen it on occasions around Beacon Hill and Botany Bay. It lays its eggs on honeysuckle.

Right: The fast flying painted lady butterfly at rest on knapweed.

Satyridae family

In a few small areas of old pastureland and grassy hillsides locally it is possible to see a few species of the brown butterflies or Satyridae. These are the **meadow brown** *(Maniola jurtina)*, **marbled white** *(Melanargia galathea)*, **ringlet** *(Aphantopus hyperantus)*, the gregarious **gatekeeper** *(Pyronia tithonus)* and the **speckled wood** *(Pararge aegeria)*.

The marbled white with its black, white-blotched wings was once known in the early 19th century as the 'half-mourner'. The term had its origins in the black and white dresses that women wore during half-mourning, the period that followed full mourning for a dead relative, when only black was worn. The gatekeeper can regularly be found feeding on Common Ragwort, a plant which is poisonous to some farm livestock but it is a great source of food to many insects.

The speckled wood can also be seen in more shady situations such as woodland rides and leafy lanes, with its brown ground-colour and yellow spots blending well with the dappled sunlight on the foliage. These spots and its connection with woods gave it another 18th century name, wood argus, after the many-eyed hero of Greek mythology. The caterpillars of all the browns eat grass, and all the species spend the winter as caterpillars, feeding during mild weather. The speckled wood may also live through the winter as a chrysalis.

Ringlet butterflies mating on heath bedstraw

Meadow brown butterfly and scorpion fly on knapweed

Gregarious gatekeepers feeding on ragwort

Right: A recently emerged female marbled white butterfly warming up

Lycaenidae family

Three small butterflies, all members of the **Lycaenidae** can be seen in the same grassy habitat as the browns. The **small copper** *(Lycaena phlaes)* a little jewel of a butterfly. It has wings the colour of burnished copper, spotted with black and edged with brown. The caterpillars feed on dock and sorrel.

The brightly coloured small copper feeding on knapweed

The **common blue** *(Polyommatus icarus)* is fairly widespread here, with the caterpillars feeding on various species of the vetch family, particularly bird's-foot trefoil.

Another of our early spring butterflies belonging to this group is the **holly blue** *(Celastrina argiolus)* which appears in late March, frequenting open woodland, hedges and gardens wherever its two food plants, holly and ivy, are present. There are two generations of caterpillars every year, both preferring the flower buds of their food plant to the leaves. The holly buds are available in spring for one generation, and the ivy buds in autumn for the other. Having different food plants at different times of the year is unique among British butterflies.

A fourth small member of the same family is the **green hairstreak** *(Callophrys rubi)*. Locally it can be seen in the scrubby areas where it lays its eggs on gorse, bilberry and bramble. It is the smallest hairstreak and the green metallic colour of the underside of the wings is unique among British butterflies. It is the only hairstreak to winter as a chrysalis, making it the first hairstreak to appear in the spring, usually in late April or early May. All other hairstreaks spend the winter as eggs.

Common blue butterfly at rest on a cat's-ear clock

Left: Speckled wood butterfly warming up on bracken

Green hairstreak butterfly on knapweed

Hesperidae family

The **large skipper** *(Ochlodes venata)* is a member of the Hesperidae and is most likely to be seen between June and August. It favours grassland where cock's-foot and other coarse grasses are present. Like some other members of the skipper family the large skipper has highly flexible forewings that can not only be raised and lowered during flight but can also be drawn backwards. It often can be seen resting with its fore-wings raised and hind-wings horizontal. The **small skipper** *(Thmyelicus sylvestris)* is often found in similar places but appears slightly later in the year.

A small skipper butterfly in its natural grassland habitat

Geometridae family and Noctuidae family

Being for the most part night-flying insects, moths are seen less often than butterflies. Although many species are brightly coloured and beautifully patterned, in general dull tones and cryptic colouring dominate, particularly when they are at rest. Interestingly, many have vernacular names that stir the imagination - like red-necked footman, setaceous Hebrew character, *merveille du jour*, peach blossom and lobster.

Over 800 species of macro moths have been identified in Britain; the two largest families being the Geometridae with over 300 species, and the Noctuidae with over 400. The Geometridae are very varied, in general having broad triangular wings and light slender bodies that facilitate low-energy flight rather than speed. The Noctuidae are in the main stout-bodied, drab, medium-sized moths with forewings that are often substantially longer than they are deep. This design makes for manoeuvrability and speed.

The **canary-shouldered thorn** *(Ennomos alniaria)* is a member of the Geometridae family. As its name suggests it has a bright fluffy canary-yellow thorax, making it one of our most attractive moths, with a wingspan of 36-42 mm. It inhabits woodland.

Another very colourful member of the same family is the **large emerald** *(Geometra papilionaria)*. This is a large green moth with a wingspan of 50-64 mm. It is characterised by its butterfly-like resting position. It also is a woodland species, and its larvae feed on beech, hazel and birch.

The striking large emerald moth amongst leaf litter

Right: The aptly named canary-shouldered thorn moth on ivy.

Moths: A Revealing Survey

During the foot and mouth epidemic of a few years back and the subsequent restrictions on access to the countryside I was unable to pursue my hobby of watching and photographing wildlife. It was a frustrating time, but on the plus side it did focus my attention on something I had long promised myself I would do one day - carry out a survey of moths in the garden. Being for the most part night flyers, moths are seen less often than butterflies.

Many moths have vernacular names that stir the imagination and which always intrigued me as a teenager. These names include *merveille du jour*, peach blossom, lobster, setaceous Hebrew character and red-necked footman. They sound more like the names and descriptions of characters in Shakespeare and mystery novels than moth names. My garden sits at an altitude of 285 metres up on a south-west facing slope of the Trellech ridge. The garden is about two acres in size and is bordered by and contains a number of deciduous trees namely, English oak, rowan, common beech, sycamore, silver birch, gean and the evergreen holly. On three sides are extensive coniferous woods in various stages of growth, together with some areas of heath and bramble. Within the garden itself there is a patch of rough grassland, some small wild pockets of fern, gorse and bilberry together with an assortment of shrubs. To aid me in the survey I purchased a 160 watt blended bulb, and at dusk this was suspended over a white sheet on which I placed some old egg cartons for the moths to alight on and hide under. The attraction of moths to light has been observed through the ages, as referred to by Shakespeare:

Thus hath the candle singed the moth

From *The Merchant of Venice* by WILLIAM SHAKESPEARE

Other documented references have been traced back to Roman times.

I started the survey one May evening, and during five sessions over the next couple of months I caught and photographed about 30 different species. Then at the end of July I caught a blue moth. I knew from the reference books that blue was a rare colour in moths, and after diligently comparing the physical characteristics, markings and time of year of its capture I was convinced it was a grass emerald. The books stated that freshly emerged grass emerald moths could be bluish green, and they also stated the green colouring was very unstable and faded fairly quickly. I spoke to several national moth experts and they agreed with my conclusion, although they had never seen a totally blue one. All of these discussions had taken place over the phone, so to finally clear up the mystery I took a colour slide of the moth to Cardiff Natural History Museum, where their resident expert confirmed it was a grass emerald, although he too had never seen or heard of a totally blue one. I suppose you have to call this discovery beginner's luck but it certainly fired my enthusiasm. I stopped trapping in mid-November after I had increased my species tally to around 80 and managed to photograph 70 of them.

One incident which still causes great amusement in the household is the time I went into the house after checking the trap and said, 'I have found an old lady in the outhouse'. There was a stunned silence, followed immediately by expressions of concern and questions as to why I had not brought her in. The atmosphere changed rapidly with everybody collapsing in laughter when I explained an old lady was a large brown moth that sometimes comes into homes, and is often found hiding behind the curtains.

A unique blue grass emerald moth at rest

The use of a blended bulb and a white sheet with no retention capability was not the most efficient way to catch moths, as many visited and then left. It was also very labour intensive needing constant surveillance. So the following spring I decided to improve my moth-trapping efficiency and bought a Skinner trap equipped with a 125 watt mercury vapour bulb. The trap is designed to attract and retain moths with the result it can be left unattended. Over the next nine months, I increased my moth species tally to 140. I should add that moths are not the only insects lured by the light; at specific times throughout the year a number of insects including burying beetles, cockchafers, mayflies, midges, caddis flies, mosquitoes, wasps, bumblebees including the small carder bee, ants and craneflies found their way into the trap. When cockchafer beetles, commonly known as 'May bugs', entered the trap they created great unrest. Being large and having armoured wing cases (elytra) they ricocheted about inside the metal-sided trap like balls on a pin table, upsetting the resting moths. They were quickly removed.

One observation I made is that moths are most active on warm, calm, overcast evenings, so these are usually the most productive. This observation is endorsed by one of nature's expert insect catchers, the common toad. These creatures were always present on such nights, sitting motionless in the grass like small statues, waiting to flick out their sticky tongue at any passing insect.

By the end of the year I was surprised to find that the overall species count was approaching 200; this figure represents about 25 per cent of the total number of macro moths to be found in the UK. I have to add that when I started this survey I never anticipated the species count would be so high and because of this it has become somewhat addictive, as each time you trap and identify a different species you think there are probably still more to find and identify. I managed to photograph about 150 of them, and all the moths were released after identification.

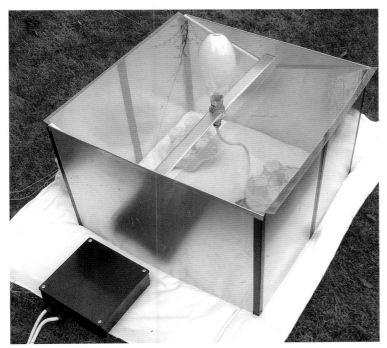

The Skinner moth trap showing the letterbox opening

My overriding impressions of the survey has been the range of rich colours and beautiful markings present. I can't help feeling that the decorative markings and colour combinations exhibited by moths must have been the inspiration behind some of the worldwide ethnic designs seen today.

A list of all the identified species has been forwarded to the Monmouthshire Lepidoptera Recorder. Moth research is on the increase in Britain, but more needs to be done in order to build up precise maps of species distribution, population trends, and possible changes in flight seasons due to global warming. There is also a need to continue to target species that are in decline and try to identify and understand the associated reasons.

A beautiful and distinctive member of this group with a wingspan of 50-64mm, is the **swallow-tailed moth** (*Ourapteryx sambucaria*). It has pale yellow, almost diaphanous wings. Two thin yellow-brown lines cross the forewings and there are two red-brown spots on each hindwing next to the swallowtails. It inhabits woods, hedges and gardens, sometimes coming to lit windows after dark. Its food plants include ivy and hawthorn.

Swallow-tailed moth on ivy covered tree trunk

Finally, there is the striking, black and white **magpie moth** (*Abraxas grossulariata*) a fairly common day-flying moth, with a wingspan of 42-48 mm, that takes its name from the bird. The caterpillars feed on hazel and hawthorn; they can be a pest in the garden where they are partial to fruit bushes.

The striking magpie moth on hazel, one of its larval food plants

There are many species of the noctuidae family, many with cryptic colouring. In the main, they are night fliers, so when they are at rest during the daylight hours on walls and tree trunks, they are extremely difficult to spot.

Two of the largest species in the family can be seen locally, namely the **old lady** (*Mormo maura*) and the **large yellow under-wing** (*Noctua pronuba*). The old lady, a mottled grey-brown colour, is so named because the top half of the forewings are covered with a marbled pattern that resembles a shawl. It has a wingspan of 64-74 mm; it sometimes finds its way into houses. The large yellow under-wing is smaller with a wingspan of 50-60 mm. The forewings vary in colour from dark or red-brown to light brown, and the under-wings are orange-yellow edged with black. It is often disturbed from ground vegetation, flying away rapidly, highlighting its brightly coloured hindwings.

Right: A group of hibernating herald moths

A particularly beautiful and uniquely marked member of this group is the ***merveille du jour** (Dichonia aprilina)*, sometimes found during the day hiding on the trunk of a tree. It flies during September and October, and feeds on over-ripe berries. Wingspan 42-52 mm.

The beautiful merveille du jour moth feeding on blackberries.

A resting silver Y moth displaying the Y marks on its forewings which gives it its common name

A very distinctive moth in this group is the **herald** *(Scoliopteryx libatrix)*. Once called the 'furbelow moth' it over-winters as an adult, sometimes in outbuildings and caves, often in large numbers. In a recent winter, a group of nine hibernated in our outhouse, appearing there in mid-September, with the last one not leaving until mid-May the following year. It is one of our longest living moths. Wingspan 44-48 mm. A day-flier of this group is the **silver Y** *(Autographa gamma)*. It varies in colour from a white-grey through various tints of grey and brown to velvet-black, with a white 'Y' in the centre of the forewing. It is an immigrant moth from southern Europe, so its numbers vary considerably. In 1987 and in 2002 they were present in large numbers in the newly planted areas on Beacon Hill and Trellech Common. They do breed in England and Wales, but winter survival is considered rare. Wingspan 32-52 mm.

The brilliant coloured knot grass moth caterpillar feeding on creeping jenny

A common mottled grey-black moth found in low vegetation and grass is the **knot grass** *(Acronicta rumicis)*. Its food plants are herbaceous and woody, including plantains and broad-leaved dock. The striking, highly coloured, hairy larva is well worth seeking out. It can be found in May-June and again in August-September. Wingspan 34-44 mm.

Right: The day flying burnet companion moth in its natural habitat, the flower meadow

Two other day-flying moths in this group that can be seen in the same flower meadow habitat are the attractive **burnet companion** *(Euclidia glyphica)* and **mother shipton** *(Callistege mi)*. Both have a wingspan of 28-34 mm. The burnet companion is so named because it is often seen together with day-flying burnet moths. It often settles, displaying its yellowy-orange/dark-brown banded hindwings.

Mother shipton derives its name from the cream-edged brown area in the centre of the forewing. This resembles a profiled caricature of an old hag with an eye and hooked nose. It was named after Old Mother Shipton, a 16th century Yorkshire witch; notoriety is perpetuated in many strange ways. The larvae feed on red and white clover and bird's-foot trefoil both can be seen in New Grove Meadows, one of Gwent Wildlife Trust's reserves just north of Trellech. These meadows probably have the finest spring displays of common spotted and green-winged orchids to be seen anywhere in Britain. It is well worth a visit to the district just to see them.

Sphingidae family

The hawk moths, all members of the Sphingidae family, are large, swift, powerful fliers with rather narrow pointed forewings and wingspans of between 60 and 100 mm. Most of their larvae are large, with striped colouring and a 'horn' at the tail end. A number of this group of moths can be seen locally, including the **elephant hawk moth** *(Deilephila elpenor*, **lime hawk moth** *(Mimas tiliae*, **poplar hawk moth** *(Laothoe populi)* **eyed hawk moth** *(Smerinthus ocellata)* and **humming-bird hawk moth** *(Macroglossum stellatarum)*.

The elephant hawk moth is probably the prettiest of the hawk moths; it is on the wing in June and can be seen in the evening feeding on honeysuckle or valerian. Rosebay willow herb is the main foodplant of the larva, which, in the fully-grown state, is a fearsome-looking brown-grey caterpillar, with two pairs of circular markings like eyes just behind the head. When disturbed it retracts

A host of common spotted orchids in the New Grove meadows reserve

Right: An eyed hawk moth exhibiting its colourful hind wings

its head into its body, causing the front portion to swell up like an elephant's head. It measures up to 80 mm in length.

The humming-bird hawk moth is a day flier and summer visitor, which migrates from the south of France where it is common. Like a humming-bird, it hovers in front of the flower, inserting its long proboscis deep into the petals to extract nectar, its wings emitting a high-pitched humming sound. They beat so fast that they are barely visible. Some people have mistaken the moth for a humming bird. There has been an increase in sightings locally over the last five years, providing possible evidence of global warming. I saw one in March 1998 making it a very early migrant, or is it possible it over wintered?

The handsome elephant hawk moth on its favoured larval food plant, willowherb

A poplar hawk moth resting and well camouflaged on a tree trunk

Lime hawk moth at rest on a tree trunk

Elephant hawk moth caterpillar feeding on willowherb

Notodontidae family

Three interesting members of the Notodontidae family that can be found locally are the **puss moth** *(Cerura vinula)*, **buff tip** *(Phalera bucephala)* and **lobster moth** *(Stauropus Fagi)*. They vary in wingspan from 55-85 mm.

The puss moth has pale grey wings finely engraved with black. Its body is covered with cat-like fluffy hair, hence its name. It is generally found between April and July in damp places where sallow, willow and poplar are present. The fully grown caterpillar is up to 65 mm long, green with a diamond-shaped area of purple-brown on its back. At the posterior are two whip-like filaments.

When alarmed it adopts a menacing attitude, the head rears up and is drawn back into the thorax, causing it to swell and present a scarlet collar coupled with two false staring eyes. At the same time the two rear filaments curl forward and two red flagella emerge, the whole presenting a fearsome presence. The well-camouflaged cocoon, built into the bark of a tree, is made up of fragments of wood, chewed up by the caterpillar and cemented together with a secretion to form a hard cocoon. The buff tip is remarkable for its highly developed and unusual camouflage pattern. When at rest with its folded silver-grey, yellow-tipped wings it resembles a piece of broken birch twig. I have seen this moth occasionally on the birch trees at Cleddon Bog.

The attractive lobster moth derives its name from the larva that has two pairs of legs longer than those of any other caterpillar, making it look like a small lobster. It grows over 50 mm long, and the tail end is held over the body scorpion fashion.

Buff tip moth in characteristic rest simulating a broken birch twig

The furry lobster moth at rest showing the hind-wings protruding under the forewings

Lasiocampidae family

Another large moth that can be seen here is the **drinker** *(Euthrix potatoria)*, a member of the Lasiocampidae family. It looks robust and varies in colour from brown to buff, frequenting tall damp grassland. The male has feathered antennae; the female is the larger with an outstretched wingspan of up to 70 mm.

The day-flying **fox moth** *(Macrothylacia rubi)* is a smaller member of the same group. It is red-brown; two pale yellow lines cross the forewings. I have never seen the moth locally, but they are about, as I have found the caterpillar a few times feeding on bramble. Wingspan 48-72 mm.

Male drinker moth at rest amongst coarse grass

Arctidae family

The **garden tiger** *(Arctia caja)*, **scarlet tiger** *(Callimorpha dominula)* **rosy footman** *(Miltochrista miniata)* and the **cinnabar moth** *(Tyria jacobaeae)* are all brightly coloured members of the Arctiidae family.

The day-flying scarlet tiger (wingspan 52-58 mm) is rarely seen here, but the garden tiger is fairly common and when seen, is instantly recognisable; its forewings are white with broad chocolate marbling, the hindwings are yellow or orange with black spots, the wingspan is 50-78 mm. The caterpillars with their coat of long brown hair are commonly called 'woolly-bears'; they feed on a wide variety of herbs.

The distinctive scarlet tiger moth at rest on bramble, one of its larval food plants

The rosy footman is a small, very attractive rosy pink moth that can sometimes be disturbed from woody vegetation and rough grass found along woodland edges and forest rides in June-August. Wingspan 25-33 mm.

The red warning patches on the wings of the day flying cinnabar moth give it its name, as they are the colour of the pigment mercuric sulphide, also known as

Right: A rosy footman moth on lichen, its larval food plant

cinnabar. The orange and black-banded caterpillars can usually be seen in July and August feeding on ragwort and groundsel, which are common along the edges of some forest rides. Wingspan 35-45 mm.

A cinnabar moth laying eggs on the underside of a ragwort leaf

Zygaenidae family

The **six-spot burnet moth** *(Zygaena filipendulae)* is a member of the Zygaenidae group of moths.t is a brightly coloured day-flying gregarious moth, with black forewings dotted with red, and red hind-wings edged with black. These moths are sluggish on the wing, and can be seen regularly from late June to August resting on the heads of wildflowers. Some of these highly coloured day-flying moths are poisonous, making them inedible to most insect-eating animals. Wingspan 30-40 mm.

A six-spot burnet feeding on knapweed

Chapter 11
Beetles *and bugs*

The beetles (order Coleoptera) are insects that can generally be described as having their forewings, or elytra, hardened into protective covers for their functional, flight hind-wings; although there are exceptions.

Cicindelidae family

There are five British species of the Cicindelidae family, commonly called tiger beetles. Two can be found locally. There is the attractive **green tiger beetle** *(Cicindela campestris)*. These are long legged, fast-running and fond of sunning themselves on the ground in early summer. They can be seen in the spring on the forest paths and rides on Trellech Hill and Beacon Hill. As their name suggests, they have a green body with yellow spots. When disturbed they take off with a noisy buzzing flight, rarely flying far. Although only 18-20 mm long, they are fiercely carnivorous.

The other species is the rarer **wood tiger beetle** *(Cicindela sylvatica)*, which is similar in size and habits, but is brown-grey with cream stripes and spots. They favour woodland.

Caribidae family

Close relatives of the Cicindelidae group are the Caribidae, commonly known as ground beetles because they spend most of their time on or under the ground. These are also good runners, but many lack wings. The elytra are fused together on certain species, which gives them added protection as they creep about amongst debris. Most ground beetles are nocturnal. During the day, they can be found in dark corners and under stones and logs. A common member of this group is the **violet ground beetle** *(Carabus violaceus)*, a large flightless insect 25-30 mm long with long legs. It is noticeably violet-black in colour, particularly towards the edges. This beetle is useful to gardeners and farmers as it consumes large numbers of plant-feeding insects.

Staphylinidae family

The Staphylinidae is another large and varied group, whose members usually have long narrow bodies and short elytra, exposing most of the abdomen. One of the species - probably the most interesting - is the **devil's coach horse** *(Ocypus olens)*. It likes damp places, lurking under stones and logs, where it reacts to disturbances by curling its tail into a scorpion-like posture. Although it looks menacing, it is quite harmless. In Irish mythology this beetle is a symbol of corruption. It is said that it will appear after dealing with the devil, and that it will eat sinners. By raising its tail, it is said to cast a curse. It is carnivorous, eating insects and spiders as well as carrion. Length 25 mm.

The long legged fast running green tiger beetle

Devil's coach horse in typical tail up attitude when feeling threatened

Silphidae family

A dead animal or bird found lying in a field, if turned over, may well reveal the presence of a pair of orange and black **sexton beetles** *(Nicrophorus vespilloides)*, commonly known as burying or grave-digging beetles.

Sexton burying beetle with dead rodent, potential host for its eggs/lava

They are members of the Silphidae group of beetles. All have strongly clubbed antennae. These beetles have a remarkably good sense of smell, and they can smell decaying carrion up to 3 km away. They work in pairs: the first to arrive at a carcass appear to fight later arrivals and turn them away.

After mating, the beetles bury the carcass, by removing the soil from beneath it, until it is completely interred. When completed, the female excavates a small passage leading away from the burial chamber and lays her eggs there, and then returns to the carcass to feed. She then stays and feeds her offspring with regurgitated food until they are able to feed on the carcass themselves. Length 20-25 mm.

Scarabaeidae family

Another large species, whose members help to keep the countryside a more pleasant place, are the Scarabaeidae family. There are two main groups - the dung beetles and the plant-eating chafers. The **dor beetle** *(Geotrupes stercorarius)* is fairly common in the area, and gets its name from its appetite for animal dung. It eats horse and cow dung, and also buries dung balls for larvae to eat. It is a glossy blue-black with ridges down the back, and 20-25 mm long. The name dor comes from an old word meaning drone, as it flies with a droning sound. Foxes regularly eat them.

Whereas the scavenging dung beetles are useful, the chafers are decidedly harmful. The largest chafer is the **cockchafer** *(Melolontha melolontha)* or maybug. Common in the area, it flies mainly at night and often comes crashing into lighted windows in early summer. These beetles cause considerable damage to trees and crops by eating the foliage and flowers. The fat, white larvae can be even more destructive, they live underground for three to four years consuming plant roots, particularly cereals and grasses. Colour: Predominately brown, black thorax and highly feathered antennae. Length: up to 35mm.

A scarce distinctive plant chafer that can be seen here is the attractive **bee-chafer** *(Trichius fasciatus)*. The whole

Right: The scarce bee-chafer feeding on yarrow

body - including the elytra - is covered with golden brown hair making it resemble a bumblebee. The elytra appear to have four large false eyes. When the feeding chafer has its head buried deep in a flowerhead, it is highly vulnerable, so these false eyes have probably evolved to present an intimidating 'keep-off' image to any other nectar-seeking insect or potential predator. The larvae feed on rotting tree stumps, particularly birch, and the adults feed on flowers. On the few occasions, I have seen them, they have been feeding on thistle, knapweed and yarrow flowers in old grassland, and on the edges of forest rides around Trellech Common and Beacon Hill.
Length 12-14 mm.

Cantharoidae family

The **soldier beetle** *(Rhagonycha fulva)* is the slender red beetle, regularly seen on umbelliferous plants such as cow parsley. Because of its colour it has earned the misleading name of 'bloodsucker' in certain parts of Britain. It is a member of the Cantharoidae super family of beetles, which are carnivorous and feed on small flower visiting insects. The soldier beetles' colour is a warning to birds that they contain distasteful chemicals and are inedible Length: 13-16 mm.

The **glow-worm** *(Lampyris noctiluca)* is one of the most famous of all insects, and a member of the same family. Years ago it was common here, but is now considered rare. It is the female that emits the pale greenish blue light. The underside of her last three abdominal segments bears the light-producing organs, which use oxygen, water and an enzyme to produce the light emitting substance, oxyluciferin. A reflector of minute crystals enhances this light. Adult glow-worms do not feed much, but the larvae feeds on small snails and slugs. The need to feed on snails tends to restrict glow-worms to areas of chalk and limestone where snails are commonest. Male brownish, 10-12 mm long; Female brown, wingless and looks more like a beetle larvae, 12-18mm long.

Cerambycidae family

Strangalia maculata beetle a pollen feeder on cat's-ears

The strikingly marked **wasp beetle** *(Clytus arietis)* is seen regularly displaying its bright pattern while running about on the leaves of shrubs. The beetle not only mimics the wasp in size, colour, and shape but also in its behaviour. It scuttles about in an agitated way tapping its antennae in the manner of a wasp. It belongs to the family of wood-feeding beetles called Cerambycidae, commonly called longhorns. They are usually recognised by their very long antennae. The adult feeds on nectar, while the larvae eat decaying wood. Two other common members of this group are *Strangalia maculata*, length 18-22mm, and *Rhagium mordax,* length 20mm.

Rhagium mordax beetle in its woodland habitat

Coccinellidae family

Several species of Coccinellidae or ladybirds are found here, including the **eyed ladybird** *(Anatis ocellata)*, Britain's largest ladybird, which is found on pine trees. They are all beneficial to man as they destroy vast numbers of greenfly and other pests. Their active little slate-blue larvae are also voracious predators of aphids, hatching out from orange-coloured eggs laid in clusters on leaves.

Hemiptera order - True Bugs

Close scrutiny of the leaves of hazel and hawthorn bushes throughout the spring and summer will often reveal the presence of two members of the true bugs - namely the **green shieldbug** *(Palomena prasina)* and the slightly larger **hawthorn shieldbug** *(Acanthosoma haemorrhoidale)*. The flat, broad bodies of these bugs, shaped like heraldic shields, give them their names. They feed by sucking the juices from leaves. Colour: green, but the hawthorn shieldbug has a red triangle on its back. Length 12-17 mm.

Another member of the group to be found in the woods is the **forest bug** *(Pentatoma rufipes)*. It is brownish bronze with an orange spot at the base of the pronotum, length 15 mm. It also feeds by sucking the juices from the leaves.

Appearing armour plated! The distinctive forest bug

Right: Green shieldbug in a typical habitat

Chapter 12
Ants, *bees and wasps*

Hymenoptera order

Ants, bees, wasps and others make up the large Hymenoptera order; this covers a wide range of form and habit, including the social mode of existence. One of the members of this group seen locally is the impressive looking **giant wood wasp** *(Urocerus gigas)* that can be up to 38 mm long. This name is misleading, as it is a sawfly. The female has a long, stout ovipositor, which gave rise to its common name of 'horntail'. On the wing it makes a distinctive buzzing sound. And presents a fearsome picture, although it is harmless. I must admit when I first saw one on Trellech Hill I had my doubts about the harmless tag! The female lays her eggs, via her ovipositor in the timber of Scots pine, larch and birch.

Several species of ant occur. Some live under stones, others under the bark of decaying logs, but the most common is the large **wood ant** *(Formica rufa)*. It is most prolific in the pine woods, particularly those in the pole-stage, where I have seen anthills of pine needles and other vegetable matter up to 1.5 metres high.

Although bumble bees appear to be declining it is still possible to see the large **buff-tailed bumblebee** *(Bombus terrestris)*, which is 16 mm long and particularly fond of visiting foxgloves. Another species - somewhat more common - is the smaller *Bombus pratorum*. Like the buff-tail, it has two yellow bands, but is only 11 mm long, and a regular feeder on cotoneaster flowers in the spring. A further species is the attractive **red-tailed bumblebee**

(Bombus lapidarius). The female can be up to 25mm long; most of the body is black, but it has a distinct red abdomen. The male is smaller; in addition to the red abdomen it has a yellow band behind the head.

The attractive red-tailed bumblebee on knapweed

A Diet of Bees

Sometimes June can be a cold, wet and windy month. This kind of weather one year led to a shortage of caterpillars with the result that the great tits and blue tits on and around Trellech Beacon had a hard time hatching and feeding their young. A number of broods failed to hatch, and two broods of great tits in nest-boxes in the garden suffered losses, being reduced from seven and eight young to three and four respectively. Walking around the garden I noticed that the adult birds from both nest-boxes were constantly flying back and forth to a berry-producing shrub *(Cotoneaster horizontali)*, an apparent source of food. A closer look revealed that the shrub was in flower and alive with bumblebees *(Bombus pratorum)*, not great tit diet, or so I thought.

Continued observation from close range showed that the birds were alighting on the shrub amongst the bees, where they selected and caught one each. They then flew immediately into an adjacent lilac bush, where they struck the bee against a branch, presumably stunning and killing it. This action was then followed by three distinctly separate operations, which appeared to entail the removal of the wings and sting from the bee. Each great tit then carried the bee to the nest, fed its young, and the cycle was repeated.

I was also surprised to find in a nest-box in which all the fledglings had died the presence of two sexton burying beetles. The box was three metres from the ground up a tree, highlighting just how efficient these beetles are at locating carrion on which to lay their eggs.

As in recent years there have been many cold springs, I have witnessed this bee eating regularly, although it only appears to happen as a last resort when there is a shortage of caterpillars.

And, of course, there is the ubiquitous **common wasp** *(Vespula vulgaris)*. Man has a love-hate relationship with these wasps. They do a lot of good in the garden in terms of the numbers of small pests, such as caterpillars and aphids, that they eat. Against this, they are a pest in the late summer when fruit is ripe, and they sting if you upset them. They live in tight-knit colonies in nests made of paper, which they manufacture, from wood. They usually build their nests underground in burrows left by small mammals, but sometimes nest in buildings. Recently a nest was built into an air vent in the loft of our house, filling the vent and extending down the inside wall. I removed the nest the following spring, and was amazed at its size, for it was about half a metre long. But the really fascinating aspect was the delicate patterning on the nest, produced by the use of several different coloured woods, a real work of art.

Insect art! A close up of a section of a common wasp nest, each coloured layer being an individual piece of chewed wood

The **hornet** *(Vespa crabro)* is the largest of our native wasps and grows to a length of 32 mm. It is becoming increasingly rare locally; probably due to the loss of old hollow trees, its natural nesting place.

Unlike the common wasps and hornets, which are highly social, the great majority of wasps are solitary, laying their eggs in single nests or in the bodies of living hosts. One such wasp found locally is the 20 mm long, orange and black-bodied **sand digger wasp** *(Ammophila sabulosa)*. It places a caterpillar it has paralysed into a burrow it has dug in light soil, then lays an egg on it and seals the burrow. The egg hatches into a grub, which proceeds to eat the live paralysed caterpillar.

Ichneumonidae family

The ichneumonidae family is a group of fairly large insects, often with large ovipositors. The most striking ichneumon fly to be seen locally and anywhere in Britain is the female *Rhyssa persuasoria,* which has a body length

The wandering broad bodied chaser which inhabits still and slow flowing water.

of 30 mm, coupled to an ovipositor up to 40 mm long. This insect parasitizes the larvae of the giant wood wasp found in the pine woods. It is able to locate the host larvae tunnelling in the tree trunks, and then proceeds to do the apparently impossible; it drives its ovipositor through the wood like a small auger. I have been fortunate to see this drilling sequence taking place, but as is often the case I never had the camera handy. One egg is laid next to each larva and the larval *Rhyssa* feeds externally on its host.

The colourful dragonflies and damselflies belong to the order Odonata. The nymphs of both live in water, hence the adults start their life close to it. The damselflies tend to remain near their breeding site throughout life but dragonflies will travel considerable distances.

It is possible to see the **common hawker** *(Aeshna juncea),* **southern hawker** *(Aeshna cyanea),* **broad bodied chaser** *(Libellula depressa)* and **common darter** *(Sympetrum striolatum)* dragonflies flying over ponds here, and also well away from water along the forest rides, woodland edges and over the young plantations. They fly with a rapid hawk-like flight, patrolling in search of small flying insects. Early in the morning before the day has warmed up it is possible to find them resting on leaves. They hold their wings out at right angles to the body. Years ago country names for the dragonfly were 'horse-stinger' or 'devil's darning needle', but they do not sting, as they have no stinging organs.

Now, when my roses are half buds, half flowers,
And loveliest, the king of flies has come,
It was a fleeting visit, all too brief;
In three short minutes he had seen them all,
And rested, too, upon an apple leaf.

From the poem *The Dragonfly* by W.H. DAVIES

Damselflies are generally found resting on vegetation by the water's edge; they are smaller, more delicate than dragonflies, with needle-thin bodies and a more fluttering, dancing flight. Like their big brothers, they are also predators, feeding in the same way, snatching their insect prey with their legs while on the wing, or pulling them off the vegetation. The two most likely to be seen are the **common blue damselfly** *(Enallagma cyathigerum)* and the **large red damselfly** *(Pyrrhosoma nymphula)*. Unlike the dragonflies, when at rest they hold their wings closed above the abdomen.

Orthoptera family

Finally, there are grasshoppers and crickets, which belong to the Orthoptera order. These are insects with enlarged hind legs for jumping. The song of these insects is their most interesting aspect, for each different species has its own individual vocal signature. This is produced by a process called stridulation, which involves the rubbing of one part of the body- the 'file' - over another part of the body known as the 'scraper'. The file is provisioned with a series of ridges that in turn strike the scraper, setting up vibrations. The process is very similar to drawing a comb over the edge of a card. In the case of the grasshopper this involves the hind-leg and forewing, whereas crickets rub the base of their forewings together.

> *The poetry of earth is never dead:*
> *When all the birds are faint with the hot sun,*
> *And hide in cooling trees, a voice will run*
> *From hedge to hedge about the new-mown mead*
> *That is the Grasshopper's. He takes the lead*
> *In summer luxury; he has never done*
> *With his delights, for when tired out with fun*
> *He rests at ease beneath some pleasant weed.*
> *The poetry of earth is ceasing never:*

From the poem *On the Grasshopper and Cricket* by JOHN KEATS

Most of our species complete their life-cycle in one year, the adults dying in the autumn leaving eggs behind

Close up of a common green grasshopper showing the comb

to survive the winter and produce the next year's insects. A few species take two years to mature, passing at least one winter as nymphs.

Grasshoppers feed on grasses and low-growing plants. and are most likely to be heard in old grassland and on warm grassy banks during the summer months. The two species most likely to be found locally are the **common field grasshopper** *(Chorthippus brunneus)*, and the **common green grasshopper** *(Omocestus viridulus)*. Both species are 20-24 mm long, the females being slightly larger than the male. The common field grasshoppers are generally a drab brown colour, but this can vary, whereas the common green grasshoppers, are usually green.

Crickets are similar in appearance to grasshoppers, but what sets them apart is their long antennae, which are usually longer than their body. They are more nocturnal than grasshoppers, and eat soft-bodied insects as well as plants. The species most likely to be heard and found locally are the **dark bush-cricket** *(Pholidoptera griseoaptera)*, which is 20 mm long, and the **oak bush-cricket** *(Meconema thalassinum)*, which grows up to 15mm.

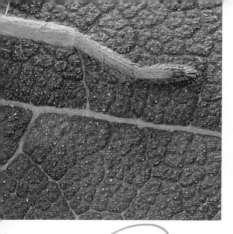

Chapter 13
Spiders

Although spiders are not true insects, it seems inappropriate not to refer to them - and I might be accused of being an arachnophobe if I didn't! Spiders are predatory, carnivorous arthropods belonging to the arachnid class of invertebrates, which is one of the oldest on the planet, stretching back 350 million years. The class is named after the mythological maiden Arachne who challenged the goddess Athena to a weaving contest and was changed into a spider. Hence, the old country superstition, *'it is unlucky to kill a spider'*. Spiders are often associated with dank, dark corners, and old, decaying buildings:

> *The bower we shrined to Tennyson,*
> *Gentlemen,*
> *Is roof wrecked; damps there drip upon*
> *Sagged seats, the creeper-nails are rust,*
> *The spider is sole denizen*

From the poem *An Ancient to Ancient*
by Thomas Hardy

Spiders can be found everywhere indoors and outdoors.

There are at least 30 family groups of spiders in Britain, composed of more than 600 species. Unlike insects, they have four pairs of legs, and do not have a larval stage. After hatching in some number from the single egg that the female of some species carry with them, spiderlings pass through several moults before they reach maturity. After hatching, the young spiderlings disperse by climbing to the top of a blade of grass, or any other high point, where they spin a single strand of silk that catches the breeze and carries them away. Spiders have only two distinct body sections - the front, covered by a tough shield or carapace that carries all the legs, there are usually eight or six eyes situated at the front. The hind section, is softer and rather bulbous.

They prey on other creatures, and it has been calculated that the weight of insects eaten by spiders every year exceeds the weight of all the humans in the world! Most spiders spin characteristic silk webs to entrap their prey, which vary in design from the classic orb web, with all its variations, the silken-lined hole and the hammock shaped designs, and webs that look like a tangled mess, resembling a knitting pattern that has gone wrong.

Each family group has its own particular design, which helps identification. Not all species produce webs, for some capture their prey by jumping on them. The best time to see the various types of web is to take an early morning walk on a bright late summer or autumn morning following a heavy dew, frost or light shower of rain. The low vegetation and hedges can be festooned with webs, highlighted by the suspended water droplets, which, when caught in the sunlight, look like jewelled necklaces. The silk strands that spiders produce are about 0.02mm in diameter, and have a breaking strain, thickness for thickness, greater than iron.

These are what I consider the most photogenic and interesting I have seen in the area:

An attractive green spider waiting to ambush passing prey

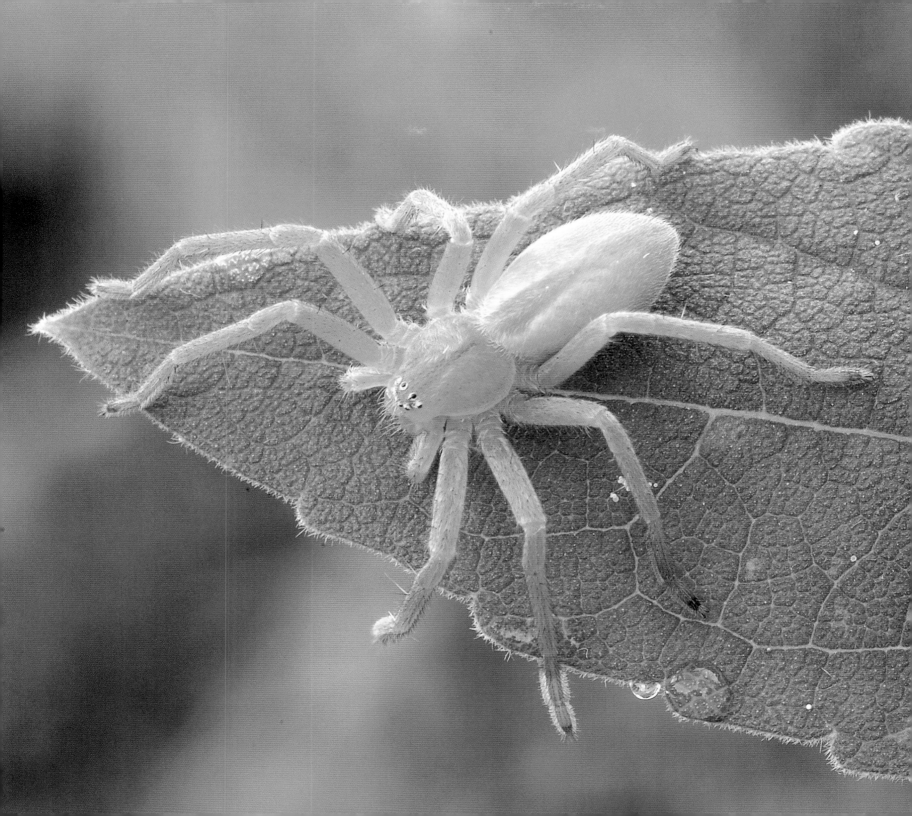

Close up of zebra spider hunting for prey on a house wall in the full heat of the sun

A little spider that is common is the brown/black and white **zebra spider** (*Salticus scenicus*) that is a member of the Salticidae family. It hunts by sight, and catches its prey by leaping on it; it can leap many times its own length. It is fully active on sunny days, when it can be seen on the walls of buildings, dry-stone walls, and fences. It is 5-7 mm long.

One of the most striking British spiders that can be seen here is the **green spider** (*Micrommata virescens*), the only member of the Micrommata genus. It has green legs and carapace, and white hairs ring the eyes. The female has a bright yellowish green abdomen, whereas the male has a yellow abdomen marked with red bands. These catch their prey by stealth, hiding in the vegetation and ambushing passing insects. I was introduced to the female of the species by a neighbour who found two of them in his flower garden. If he is keeping any other gaudy females at the bottom of his garden he's being very tight lipped about them! Length male 7-10 mm, female 10-15 mm.

The **crab spider** (*Misumena vatia*), a member of the Thomisidae family, is another eye-catching spider. It is commonly called a crab spider because its first two pairs of legs are longer than the rest, and it can walk sideways as well as backwards and forwards. These spiders can be found in summer, sitting in flowers, usually yellow or white varieties, where they wait to ambush visiting insects. They have the ability to change colour to match that of the flower it is hiding on. Colours of white, yellow, light green and a pale slate blue have been recorded. Males are 3-4 mm long, females 9-11mm.

One of the spinners of the wonderful orb webs is a member of the Araneidae family *Araneus diadematus* sometimes known as the **garden spider**. I have seen their webs up to 25-35 cm. in diameter. These webs can be found almost anywhere in hedges, low vegetation, woodland and gardens. The spiders are pale brown to black in colour with a variable white cross on the abdomen. The male is 4-8 mm long, the female 10-13 mm.

Spider's Defence

Looking out of the kitchen window one day I noticed a spider had spun a vertical orb web near one corner of the frame. As I was looking at it the flapping wings and tail of a great tit, which must have been hunting for insects on the wall and window surround, appeared in the same corner of the window. The next instant a garden spider scuttled from its unseen resting place into the centre of the web. I assumed the air currents generated by the bird's flapping wings had vibrated the web, triggering the spider to rush out in anticipation of a meal. What happened next was fascinating.

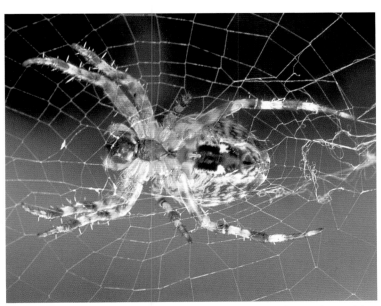

A close up of the underside of the female garden spider
showing the epigyne

which took place over a period of less than ten seconds was extremely fortuitous. I would add that this observation took place at a distance of about one metre.

This species of orb-weaving spider is often known as the 'garden spider'. Although it is not uncommon in the garden, it is more usually associated with heathland vegetation. I wonder if this is a new piece of hitherto unseen spider behaviour?

Having reached the centre of the web, the fully extended spider, having now presumably seen the great tit, went into what appeared to be a high-speed spin. All I could see was a 'brown blur' which looked like a spinning brown disc approximately 15 mm in diameter. This movement went on for several seconds during which time the great tit departed. When the movement stopped, I concluded the spider could not have been rotating through 360 degrees as this would have destroyed the web. It must have been rocking rapidly to and fro in the vertical axis like the rotary pendulum in a watch.

Knowing that spiders have hollow multi-jointed legs that not only flex but can also be extended and retracted hydraulically, I assumed it achieved this rotary rocking movement by a combination of flexing and extension/retraction of the requisite legs. This response by the spider was obviously a sophisticated, instinctive 'defence mechanism' which in this instance was successful. To witness this combination of events,

The wonder of the world,
the beauty and the power,
the shapes of things,
their colours, lights, and shades;
these I saw.
Look ye also while life lasts.

ANONYMOUS

Appendix

Photography of wildlife

I do not think this book would be complete without a few words on photography but I am not going to bore you with all the technical jargon. Many books have been written on the subject, see Bibliography. Studying these books will help you to acquire the necessary techniques. But it is imperative that you are self critical of your work, taking every opportunity to compare your results with other people's.

The idea of a wildlife photographer wandering around the countryside armed with a camera fitted with a long telephoto lens taking shots at will could not be further from the truth. The best wildlife pictures are usually the result of a detailed knowledge of the subject, planning, and patience and determination, coupled with an element of luck. Luck plays a very large part when high-speed movement, such as wing flapping, is involved. In these situations you never know what you have captured on film until you see the final picture. The result often ends up like the old adage 'the thrill of the chase is better than the catch'.

Despite these difficulties there can be few thrills more exhilarating after a long wait for the appearance of a bird or animal than pressing the shutter and later finding you have captured a magical moment.

I have recently moved into digital photography, so it is early days for making sweeping judgements, but I can already see some of the advantages of being able to view the results immediately. Yet there are shortcomings. As the inbuilt monitor is small, it is often difficult to make a precise judgment on the sharpness of focus and the presence of fine detail that are necessary for a good wildlife picture. This is particularly true of outdoor close-ups of insects, where depth of field is so critical. Consequently you need to download the picture into a computer before you can draw any final conclusions as to its acceptability, but waiting time is reduced.

The big advantage for wildlife photographers is that the size of the electronic light sensor means the focal length of the fitted lens is increased. For example the Nikon and Canon digital single-lens reflex sensors increase the focal length by approximately one and a half times, so that, for example, a 300 mm lens becomes the equivalent of a 450 mm lens. Despite this advantage - and the ability to erase instantly unwanted

pictures - I still think digital technology has some way to go to produce raw data with the sharpness of a 100 ASA film such as Fuji's Provia 100F slide film.

With digital photography, there does seem to be an unnatural smoothness and softness at the edges of the subject matter in some cases. Something appears to be lacking, and digital appears more sensitive to lighting conditions. I wonder whether a discontinuous grid made up of individual light sensors, however small, can ever achieve the same results as a continuous film emulsion, but as I said it is early days and I am on a learning curve.

Even so, the quality of a digital picture can be enhanced by a variety of highly sophisticated computer programs. The computer is rapidly replacing the darkroom for many photographers.

Finally, do remember that some species are protected against disturbance under the Wildlife and Countryside Act, which can mean a licence, is needed to approach and photograph them at certain times of the year. The Countryside Council issues these licences, but applicants have to provide evidence of competence in wildlife photography.

There is one hard and fast rule, whose spirit must be observed, and that is that the welfare of the subject is paramount, and more important than the photograph.

Suggested camera equipment

1) 35mm Single-lens reflex with TTL metering. It is probably best to choose from Canon, Minolta, Nikon or Pentax.
2) Telephoto lens focal length 300 mm or 400 mm.
3) Zoom lens nominal 80-200.
4) Micro lens 100 mm.
5) Wide-angle lens nominal 28-70.
6) Teleconverter x 1.4 or 2.0.
7) Electronic flash unit.
8) Heavy duty tripod with pan-and-tilt head.
9) A remote or cable release for the camera.

Before you buy, consider the fact that the camera records the image but the quality of the image is dependent on the lens which transfers the image. It is always best to purchase the best lens you can afford.

Glossary

Arachnid - a class of arthropods distinguished from the insects by the possession of four pairs of walking legs.

Arachnophobe - a person who has an abnormal fear of spiders.

Autotomy - the capacity to lose a portion of the body, such as limb or the tip of the tail, and grow it again, for example lizards' tails and lobsters' claws.

Crepuscular - becoming active at twilight or before sunrise.

Cryptic colouring - development by an animal of a colour pattern which conceals it against its background.

Carapace - a hard outer covering over the upper surface of the thorax.

Cere - wax-like skin which covers the base of the upper mandible.

Corvid - member of the crow family.

Coverts - covering feathers.

Crypsis - camouflage.

Decurved - downward curving.

Diurnal - occurring or active in daytime rather than at night.

Ecologist - a person who studies relationships between organisms and their environment.

Elytra - toughened hard forewings which cover the abdomen.

Epigyne - a hardened, external structure associated with reproductive organs of female spiders.

Flagella - long thin whip-like appendages.

Furbelow - a ruffle or flounce on a garment or small showy piece of ornamentation.

Gorget - a band or patch of distinctive colour on the throat of a bird.

Hibernaculum - a case, covering or structure in which an organism remains dormant for a winter.

Insectivorous - insect eating.

Instinct - innate behaviour of animals as distinct to learned behaviour, resulting from internal and/or external stimuli.

Irruption - a mass migratory movement taken at irregular intervals; in Britain usually involves birds from northern Europe like crossbills and waxwings.

Metamorphosis - the change in both form and structure which occurs when the larval form of an animal changes into the adult one, for example a tadpole into a frog.

Myxomatosis - a virus disease of rabbits introduced into England, probably from France, by unknown causes in the autumn of 1953, and spreading throughout Britain almost wiping out the rabbit population.

Neuroptera - an order of slender, weakly flying insects with relatively large net veined wings closing over their backs such as alder flies and lacewings.

Nidifugous - describes ground-nesting birds whose young leave the nest shortly after they hatch.

Oil gland - oil-secreting gland at the base of a bird's tail; the bird uses the secretion to waterproof its feathers - the scientific name is the uropygial gland.

Oviparous - producing eggs that hatch outside the body.

Ovoviviparous - producing eggs that hatch within the body.

Ovipositor - a specialised egg-laying organ in insects.

Parthenogenesis - reproduction without fertilization.

Phylloscopus - a genus of warblers.

Primaries - main flight feathers projecting along the outer edge of a bird's wing.

Pronotum - a shield-like plate covering the top of the thorax

Ride- an open unmade track through a wood.

Secondaries - shorter flight feathers projecting along the inner part of the edge of a bird's wing.

Sloughing - the shedding of the outer skin by a snake or amphibian.

Striated - striped

Sylvia - a genus of warblers.

Tragus - a projection of skin-covered cartilage in front of the opening of the external ear.

Umbeliferous - bearing umbels, a flat topped flower cluster in which the individual flower stalks arise from about the same point e.g carrot or cow parsley.

Vertebrates - have the most advanced and sub-phylum of the animal kingdom, all of whose members have their central nerve - cord enclosed in a bony or cartilaginous spine or back bone and their brain enclosed in a skull.

Vinous - colour of wine.

Bibliography and suggested reading

Field and identification guides

Cramp, S. *The Birds of the Western Palaearctic*, Oxford University Press, 1977 onwards.

Heinzel, H., Fitter, R. and Parslow, J. *The Birds of Britain and Europe*, Collins, 1973.

Campbell, B. and Ferguson-Lees, J. *A Field Guide to Birds Nests*, Anchor Press, 1972.

Macdonald, D. Barrett, P. *Mammals of Britain and Europe*, HarperCollins, 1993.

Arnold, N.Ovenden, D. *Reptiles and Amphibians of Britain and Europe*, HarperCollins, 2002.

Chinery, M. *Field Guide to the Insects of Britain and Northern Europe*, Collins, 1973.

Gibbons, B. *Field Guide to Insects of Britain and Northern Europe*, Crowood Press, Ltd. 1995.

Higgins, L.G. and Riley, N.D. *A Field Guide to the Butterflies of Britain and Europe*, Collins, 1976.

Carter, D. J., Hargreaves, B. *Caterpillars of Britain and Europe* Harper Collins, 1994.

South, R. *The Moths of the British Isles* (Edn. 4) Vol. 1 (Edited and revised by H.M. Edelston and D. S. Fletcher); Vol. 2 (Edited and revised by H. M. Edelston , D.S. Fletcher and R.J. Collins) Frederick Warne & Co reprint 1980.

Skinner, B. *Colour Identification Guide to Moths of the British Isles,* London, 1984.

Horton, G.A. *Monmouthshire Lepidoptera - The Butterflies and Moths of Gwent*, Comma International Biological Systems, 1994.

Chinery, M., General Editor, *The Natural History of Britain and Europe*, Kingfisher Books, 1982.

Guides to photographing wildlife and natural history

Richards, M. *The Focal Guide to Bird Photography*, Focal Press, 1980.

Campbell, L. *The RSPB Guide to Bird and Nature Photography*, David & Charles, 1990.

Peterson, 'Moose' B. *Nikon Guide to Wildlife Photography*, Silver Pixel Press, 1993.

Angel, H. *Photographing the Natural World*, Collins & Brown, 1994.

Angel, H. *Outdoor Photography 101 Tips and Hints*, Silver Pixel Press, 1998.

Hicks, P. *Photographing Butterflies and other Insects*, Fountain Press, 1997.